BREAK FREE FROM YOUR
DIRTY LITTLE SECRETS

A New You in 10 Secret-Breaking Stages

GRETCHEN HYDO

Break Free From Your Dirty Little Secret

Gretchen Hydo
Los Angeles, CA
Coach@GretchenHydo.com

Ordering Information:
Special discounts are available on quantity purchases by corporations, associations, educational institutions, and others. For details, contact Gretchen Hydo above.
Printed in the United States of America
First Edition
Hardcover ISBN 978-1-5136-9935-6
Softcover ISBN 978-1-5136-9934-9
eBook ISBN 978-1-5136-9933-2
Library of Congress Control Number: 2022949506

Publisher
Winsome Entertainment Group LLC
Sandy, UT

To Grammy, my guardian angel, who always said I could.
May you and your secrets rest in peace.

To all the women who still have secrets,
and to all the women who have done the work to let them go,
I thank you.

"Of all the female sins, hunger is the least forgivable; hunger for anything, for food, sex, power, education, even love. If we have desires, we are expected to conceal them, to control them, to keep ourselves in check. We are supposed to be objects of desire, not desiring beings."
Laurie Penny
Unspeakable Things

"For every woman who has ever felt like she is not enough, Gretchen's 10-Stage Secret-Breaking system is a MUST read! This is more than a book. It is a journey. It is a journey for any woman ready to change. As even one woman changes, the world changes. Knowing this, I am so grateful."

~**Iyanla Vanzant**, Spiritual Life Coach, Executive Producer, Host of *Iyanla Fix My Life*

"Gretchen Hydo has tapped into an incredibly important and transformative process which she effortlessly details in Break Free from Your Dirty Little Secrets, *with tremendous humor and wisdom. In her matter-of-fact unique brilliant voice, Gretchen makes things very simple: you CAN live the life you want; just put in the soul-searching work she outlines and follow her guidance. I love this book!"*

~**Mayim Bialik,** Ph.D., CLEC, Actor, Host of *Mayim Bialik's Breakdown*

"Who doesn't have secret shame? Whether something happened in grade school or just last week, these dirty little (or big) secrets become our masters, driving us to hide in shadows when what we really need to do as women is shine. Gretchen's book gives us a beautiful 10-step guide to overcome that prison of dark secrecy. You will love her revealed stories and those of fellow sisters, who have done worse than you can probably imagine, and you'll realize it's finally safe to let go of those secrets that have held you back. Read this book and let it change your life forever."

~**Sue Ann Pien**, Actor and Filmmaker

"Gretchen Hydo has written a powerful, vulnerable book for women that provides compassionate and practical tools to release shame and old belief systems and find spiritual and personal freedom to last a lifetime."
~**Steve Chandler,** "The most powerful public speaker in America today," best-selling author of 30 books in 25 languages, including *The Prosperous Coach* and *Time Warrior*

"Gretchen Hydo is a rare combination of compassion and grit who has transformed her secrets and emerged as a true leader for other women to do the same. If you're ready to let go of the prison of your past and live a life where you can love, shine, and grow then read this book. Do the deep work. And let Gretchen be your trusted guide as you travel the path to your New You!"
~**Melissa Ford,** Certified Intentional Prosperity Coach, Author of *Living Service: The Journey of a Prosperous Coach*

"With compassion, wisdom, and practical know-how, Master Coach Gretchen Hydo shows you how to break free from the shackles of shame and pain that come from toxic secrets of the past and boldly step into the beauty and power of your true self. This book is a huge gift of empowerment for women!"
~**Diana Long,** The Results Expert, master coach, and MFT

"Break Free From Your Dirty Little Secrets *is filled with honest, vulnerable stories from so many women, including the author, who have been holding on to secrets for years. Gretchen Hydo's 10-Stage Secret-Breaking System allows them to release the shame of these long-kept secrets so they can stop hiding and finally live the life that they were meant to live.*"

~**Susan M. Barber,** former Fortune 500 director, author of *The Visibility Factor*

"*Secrets–such a taboo and sensitive subject. We've all lived with and suffered the agony of keeping secrets. Master Coach Gretchen Hydo not only divulges her biggest, most heart-wrenching secret, but she also takes you on a journey to the other side through her recovery. Hydo has written a step-by-step guide for breaking free of your secrets and the associated low self-esteem. This book is relatable and shares the stories of many other women and their secrets. If you are ready to shed troublesome secrets and let go of the past, this book is a must read!*"

~**Karen Davis,** co-author of *How to Get the Most Out of Coaching, A Client's Guide for Optimizing the Coaching Experience*

TABLE OF CONTENTS

INTRODUCTION

Millions of women are, and will remain, secret-keepers. I too was a Class-A, crash-and-burn, champion secret-keeper and almost lost out on an exquisite life. Women are suffering globally from the shame of their secret actions, confused about their value and self-worth, and unaware that what drew them to create secrets in the first place was not their fault. We have been told how to dress, talk, act, behave, beg, wish, hope, bully, and plead for most of what we receive, even in this modern-day world. Secrets—big and small—are created every minute of every day because we have not learned how to flip the switch that stops the endless cycle.

I know we haven't met, so I am asking a lot for you to trust me. I have witnessed firsthand from the depths of the human heart every secret at the back of this book. I have talked countless women through the pain and fear they feel at the prospect of their secret getting out. I know about wanting to feel different, be different, look different. I know what it's like for my skin not to fit right. I know about being sick in my head and sick in my body. I understand why, as women, we feel compelled to act out, be brazen and then fold up to be small. I know about keeping secrets to look good, to fit in, to cover my butt, and save myself from embarrassment. If you're nodding your head, maybe you know something about this too.

We create versions of ourselves to feel safe, loved, and valued because how would we know that there is another choice?

We all have a story to tell, and it's not what the critical narrator in your head is saying to you. Our conditioned programming learned during childhood needs rewiring. Our stories hold our past, they direct us toward our future. The secrets we've collected are like suitcases full of weights that we've been carrying around, making it hard to move forward. We don't want to keep dragging them with us from place to place. We'd like to let them go, but can we haul them out to the trash and just throw them away? For so many of us, sadly, the answer is no. Your secrets are like the dress you have worn too many times, but you keep because of all the compliments you get when you wear it. Ladies, the world is your oyster. You don't need validation. You need to dump your secrets. We're beyond tired from carrying them around, and it's not surprising when I tell you, you've been held back from the life that waits for you.

As a Master Certified Coach and mentor, my deepest desire and purpose comes from partnering with others to help them uncover who they are, move through transitions, and reach their next levels of spiritual, emotional, physical, and mental satisfaction and wellbeing. No matter where they want to focus, all change starts with telling the truth, getting honest, and being willing and bold enough to let go of the old outer and inner layers of identity that the mind has created to keep us safe.

When I applied my expertise, along with my 10-Stage Secret-Breaking System, specifically to secret-keeping women, they created and stepped into deeply fulfilling lives full of truth and freedom, that they are proud of. These women did the work of breaking down their secrets, the stories and persona of the false self, and gave themselves the gift of slowing down and getting honest so that they could explore and usher in, their truest self. They've followed a roadmap that has allowed them to let go of their false self and live in their New You. A

You that uses her voice, lives unashamed, connects with others, and doesn't hide from her secrets.

With each stage of the Secret-Breaking System, the false self dissipates and withdraws the power she has had over your life. The new self emerges, leaving users of the system, beautifully whole. Unveiling your secrets has power. When light is shined on those seemingly dark places, women break free, and they flourish. When the world offers a new level of hope for one woman, everyone around her benefits tenfold. Possibility and hope are contagious. The question of *"Who is going to let me?"* becomes *"No one is going to stop me."*

This book was put into my heart many years ago, while I was walking in the park and letting inspiration find me. I had just listened to another woman share about the misery and devastation she was feeling as the result of the story she was telling herself about who she was because of a secret action she had taken a decade before. She was sure that she could never let it go. She was not the first woman I had encountered who wanted to move forward but felt unable to because of being chained to the past of her secrets.

I reflected on my own secrets and the work I have done to let go of my false identity and small living. Over lunch that day at a Mexican restaurant, I told my husband, with conviction, that I was going to write this book and create an organized system that any woman can use to break free from her secrets. I knew the system had to be easy to follow but pack a punch all at the same time. I knew the secret stories had to be intriguing and revealing so that women could see themselves inside the pages. As a woman, I also understood that women are busy and that they need an efficient process that produces results. That's what I've created and am offering to you. A place to be known. A place to be seen. A place where you know you aren't alone and your feelings are shared by other women. My heart has room to hold and to give space to you, special you, so that you can begin to find your way back to yourself—to who you were before you were afraid, unsure, and a secret keeper.

As you read this book, know that you're not alone. You're surrounded by a group of women who've put their hearts on the line for you so that you feel supported as you do this work. You are not unlovable. You are not bad. You are enough. You are right where you're supposed to be. Think of me as a trusted confidant who is going to love you when you feel unlovable. I've been in your shoes and walked the thousand-mile path to become secret-free. I know what it takes to get from where you are now to where you want to be. And I intend to show you the way. My greatest healing came from being able to look people in the eye, tell my truth, and admit that I had no idea what to do. That's where the path forward started for me. It's where transformation took root, fear slipped away, and a freer way of living emerged.

Like a train leaving the station, this book will take you for a ride through the journey of who you were and how you became the woman you are now and will lead you to the woman that you are meant to be. My 10-Stage Secret-Breaking System is for every woman, *myself included*, who has lived, loved, failed, and is ashamed even if she can't identify the feeling of shame. You are tired of hiding behind the walls of your story, embarrassment, false truths, and lies. You harbor a glimmer of hope that there is another way—another life you're meant to live—but you feel exhausted, helpless, and alone. The time is here to change, and the solution is in this book. Be open and curious to the possibilities of what's to come, because sister, something amazing is around the corner for you.

My book is an anthem for you, and all women who are ready to break free from the shame they've been holding because of their secrets. It is an antidote to give voice to the truth. It is a gong of encouragement to end the cycle of secret-keeping, shame, and small living.

The time has come to let the cat out of the bag, ladies. It's time to tell your secret.

STAGE ONE

Calling Out Your Secret

Every single one of us has a secret—a dirty little secret that we're hiding to protect us, help us get ahead, or be loved. No matter its scope or the number—big or small, two or ten—women hold their secrets deeply within, and they chip away at who we are and keep us from living a life full of purpose. Secrets rob us of our authenticity and cut us off from our true selves. When we live like that, we are ripped off and so is the world, because it never receives our gift of wholeness. Ladies, the time has come to release your secrets, shed the tears, and start living the life intended for your beautiful greatness.

Secrets deliver a one-two-three punch. The first swing is the secret action, which becomes "the secret;" the second jab is the false story that you now tell yourself about who you are because of the secret action and the secret (e.g., I am the worst kind of worst because I had an affair and, therefore, am inherently untrustworthy for life), and the knock-out punch is the why behind the secret action—ultimately the" big secret" (e.g., childhood conditioning and faulty wiring taught you low self-esteem and the belief there isn't enough love to go around for you). It's exhausting living life in the boxing ring.

The more secret actions you take, the more you fuel shame, self-punishment, the critical narrative, feelings of unworthiness or self-righteousness, and on and on and on. Like a leaky faucet, secret-keeping drains us of our power, one secret at a time. Secrets change the way we view ourselves and the world, giving us a dimmer vision of who we are and what we're meant to do. They keep us in place and on the sidelines of our life. We've been conditioned to keep secrets to play it safe, but it's time to rise and break free from secrets.

Secrets compete for our attention. Because we are compelled to conceal them, we divide our time between protecting our secrets and living authentically. This contradiction leaves us depleted and lacking focus on where we could be expanding our life. Once we open the door to secret-keeping, we become a slave to them and begin collecting and creating more so that we can try to quench their insatiable thirst to not be found out. We also must face the demons behind the big secret so that we can live in our true selves.

This entangled web, in which so many women find themselves trapped, is why I created the Secret-Breaking System, a 10-Stage process to help women break free from their secrets and the shame that keeps them handcuffed to smaller living. How you call out your secrets and process the bigger false story you have been telling about yourself is a cornerstone to finding freedom and happiness.

I know it's a shocker, but your life doesn't have to be filled with secrets! You can learn how to behave with integrity and have confidence in your worthiness, but before you get to that place of freedom, you have to call out your secret, unwire your thinking, feel your feelings, meet your false self face-to-face, and learn why you created secrets in the first place. The Secret-Breaking System, when followed, will give you a new level of understanding about who you are and what motivated and caused you to become a secret-keeper in the first place. Once you face yourself, new life will emerge.

You might be thinking, *I don't know, Gretchen. I don't think it's a good idea to start calling out my secrets. If you knew what I've done, you'd agree.* Or, *my secrets aren't a big deal. I've never cheated on anyone or stolen any money. What I'm hiding is no one's business.* But, you've picked up the book, so keep reading. You've been called here, and I'd hate to see you go.

Here's something that isn't so obvious. Secrets aren't only about what you've done—the body shaming, the abortion, the lies, and hidden unkindness. That's just the subject matter. At their core, secrets are the storage bin of hidden beliefs we hold about ourselves that we keep based on the tainted actions that we've taken. The way we view and think about ourselves is the most damaging part of our secret. These judgments become the internal critical narrative that creates our life. Gulp! I know, when I learned this, it hit me smack in the face. I had no idea that the secret was anything more than what I'd done, but the truth is I've spent more time hiding the story I've created around who I am because of the secret than about the secret itself. I've spent more time protecting the reason that I created my secrets in the first place than I have worrying about the secret actions that I've taken.

What about you? Are you stuck in the critical narrative of the story you've created about who you are because of the action behind a secret? I understand if you don't know yet for sure. Here's what I bet: your secrets have taken their toll. The replaying, thinking, and framing of the secret has made it become dirty and created a spin cycle of negative feelings that you are stuck in.

Women are a powerful, beautiful, creative, loving species. Every time we listen to our critical narrative, we diminish ourselves by living up to our tainted beliefs about who we are because of our secret. We are harsher and more punishing in our view than anyone else would be. When life is created from a critical narrative, instead of expanding, we retract. When we retract, we look for protection and lean on our secrets to keep us safe, thus creating a false version of who we are. Our false self. In this false you, the beliefs you hold about yourself because of your secrets have taken root and sprouted. The more you believe the lies about you, the farther away you get from your true self. This is the severity of secrets. They strip away our core and brainwash us to believe their mistruths. And as in everything, we live up to what we believe, and we've paid the price for our limited view.

 Secrets are the storage bin of hidden beliefs we hold about ourselves that we keep based on the tainted actions that we've taken.

Through the 10-Stage Secret-Breaking System and the identification with the stories of other women including mine, I intend to help you break free from the shame of your secrets, unravel your feelings, and live in your true self. Cleaning up the secrets and dealing with the feelings and their root cause is what's been missing from your life and perpetuating a tricky secret-keeping cycle. Because of the feelings that our secrets create, we're afraid (even if we don't see it as fear) and we live safe instead of inviting life in with childlike curiosity and wonder.

- We take the job that pays the bills instead of going for the dream that we would like to make a job.

- We stay with the guy who's nice enough but not our true equal because we don't want to be alone.

- We don't speak up or speak too loudly.

- We're too much or too little.

Flip the coin, heads or tails.

We keep our secrets quiet until the pattern calls us back and then we cheat on the nice guy, or we steal office supplies from that easy job. A little spark, a little dip, back into the darkness. Left unattended, secret creating and keeping becomes a pattern and a way of life that gives full cart blanche to our false self. Enough is enough. You don't have to keep living like this. You are stronger than your secrets. You can break your secret-keeping pattern. We will do it together.

Even though you think your secret is unique, it's not. There's nothing new under the sun. It's all been done before: the keying the car, the one-night stand, the shoplifting. All of it. While the details may differ, the feelings of needing to save our face and our ass are the same when we secret-keep. Embarrassment, astonishment, *did I actually do that*, and the *oh my God, yes, I did* moments are the same for everyone. Desperation, denial, remorse, check those off the list. The *what do I have to do to get out of this* and *no one can ever know* defense mechanism kicks in and starts protecting us.

Fear and shame about our secrets have driven all of us out of our minds. We've done, said, and thrown things that we wished we hadn't. We've demoralized ourselves for love, acceptance, money, attention and to feel safe. We hold that secret tight and make a new secret on top of the secret.

Is this starting to make more sense?

Here's just a handful of secrets I've heard from hundreds of women in my professional and personal life as a Master Certified coach, trainer, and mentor:

- Hooked up with the UPS guy in the storage closet at work

- Made up employment or degree on a resume

- Secret crush on the boss

- Embezzled money from the workplace

- Lied about your age on a dating app

- Stuffed down social anxiety with cake

- Used roommate's vibrator (yup)

- Lied so that someone wouldn't be mad

- The abortion

- Shoplifted

- The threesome

- The drunk night in jail

- Prostituting oneself (happens all the time in more ways than you think)

- Yelled at your kid too loud or spanked too often

- Hated your spouse

- Hated yourself

- Racked up debt

- Violent toward others

- Violent toward yourself

- Wanted more but thought you deserved less

- Slept with your teacher or your kid's teacher or husband's best friend, sister or dad

- Breaking and entering (drop the mic)

- Got a tattoo. Regretted tattoo. Drank over the tattoo

- Had a crush on your best friend's boyfriend or husband (come on ladies, all of us?!)

- And on and on and on

Large or small, silly or serious, we've all been conditioned to hide our secrets. And we let them define us. We lean into our secrets, the story, the drama, the shame and get comfortable. Our dirty little secrets are serious business because they have tentacles that lead to keeping more secrets so that we can keep ourselves from public embarrassment and shame. No matter how we hide our secrets, we are left to manage their side effects—the lies that they tell us about who we are because of what we've done, the way they make us feel and behave, and the way they inevitably keep us isolated or playing small in one or more area of life. We may think that we have a handle on our secrets and that we've compartmentalized them so that they aren't hurting us or anyone else, but we are wrong. They bleed over, stack up, and take up mental storage, leaving us with no extra room or capacity.

The secret actions that we've committed need to be called out so that we don't internalize them and turn them into feelings that our critical narrator can use against us. Let me break it down. The way you treat your partner, the mean comment you said to your kid, the cruel internal thoughts about someone else, the car that you bumped into when you were parallel parking and didn't leave a note, the grapes you ate while you were shopping and didn't pay for, the last drink you had that became one too many before you got behind the wheel, are the first part of the dirty secret one-two-three punch and absolutely need to be called out.

The second part of the punch is the story that your critical narrator says about who you are because of what you've done. It's the story that the mind makes up that embeds itself into becoming a bigger secret than the action itself because the critical narrator ends up being the navigator of your life. If it decides that you aren't good enough because of the action, then it creates evidence to make the narrative true and keep you from taking chances, living authentically, and following your true north.

The three is the reason you created secrets in the first place and comes from a long-standing belief that was implemented in childhood.

Secrets deliver a one-two-three punch.
The secret action, the story you now tell
yourself about who you are, and the
"Big Secret" you hide.

Take stealing the grapes. That is your secret action, the "part one" of the secret. The critical narrative, part two, might be that you now believe that you are a thief and can't be trusted and because of that, you avoid situations where you might be put in positions of authority or where you might be put in charge of any money. Your critical narrator has created a reality where you aren't trustworthy. The second part of the punch is far more damaging than the first because it roots itself and becomes an intrinsic piece of your makeup and your mind then navigates your life based on beliefs it's created about who you are because of the action that you took. Then three, the reason that you took the action in the first place, comes from a deep-seated belief that was planted in childhood. In the case of the grapes, it might be that being sneaky and not getting caught means that you're clever, and being clever was praiseworthy.

Let's take a bigger event than stealing grapes. Let's say the secret action is that you had an affair. The critical narrative might be that you are unable to be faithful and are unworthy of a loving partnership. The third punch is the deepest part of your secret, and in this case, it might be because of your low self-esteem and the belief that was planted somewhere in childhood that there is not enough love to go around, you better take what you can get. That becomes the "big secret." Yes, your secret action was the affair, but your deeper secret is that you believe you are unworthy of a loving relationship. Most woman never dig deep enough to find parts two and three and they continue their secret-keeping cycle through most of their adulthood.

No woman is ever going to lead with, *Hi, I'm Kelly and I cheated on my husband because deep down, my low self-esteem has me blow up healthy loving relationships because, at my core, I believe there isn't enough love to go around.* No, instead we justify our actions, blame others, and live a false life because of our secrets.

No matter how your secret manifests there is a part of you that swings on the pendulum of superiority or inferiority because of your secret. You are either better than someone else or less than because of what you've done and the critical narrative you've created about it.

Regardless of where you fall, there is a small voice inside of you that is troubled. She wants more and can't figure out no matter how many

13

cleanses, therapists', Pilates instructors, yoga retreats, and meditation classes she takes why she can't get it quite right. And let's face it, you aren't a total mess who is sitting around obsessing about your secrets daily. You might not even think of them very often at all. Your life looks pretty good. You might have a career, a relationship, kids, a good enough place to live, and an education. You know how to do your hair and which pair of jeans make your butt look the best and still you wonder. *Is this it?*

Because so much of your life has been spent consciously or unconsciously protecting your secrets, your false self has taken the lead. The feeling that life somehow isn't right and that something is missing is real. It's your true self whispering to you from behind the lies. Every time you have that gnawing feeling, your true self is trying to emerge, but the false self has been leading the way for so long that your true self isn't sure how to show up even though she knows there's more. It's a back and forth, tug-of-war in your mind between the true and false self. One side wants more and the other doesn't know if you deserve it. One is ready to jump in and the other says, *not you. You don't get to live free. Not after what you've done.*

So, you run. Figuratively and mentally. You run for your thighs, and you run from your lies. You keep busy. You keep it together. There's nothing to see here. The battle becomes not wanting anyone to look too closely and desperately wanting someone to notice. Your true self wants to be vulnerable, to go deeper, to connect more with your friends, your partner, your kids, and yourself. But you don't know how because your false self hasn't let you, and you don't have time to figure it out on your own. That's why you're here and reading this book.

Beautiful woman, you're smart and have already lived through many challenges. You can stop the lies and say goodbye to your false, secret-keeping self. We are going to take this one stage at a time.

Secrets are entangled with our early conditioning. That's what drives us to create more secrets. Stay with me for a minute. I have my own dirty little secret that I'll share with you. We are going to dissect it, trace its roots, and expose its reach so that you can see all of the areas of my life the "big secret" affected. You will be amazed by its tentacles. As you see my secret play out, you can apply it to your own through the ten stages in this book. And as you apply my system to your own secret, you will start to deconstruct your false self.

For Stage One, Calling Out Your Secret, I will ask that you choose one secret action that you would like to become free from. Maybe it's the one secret you hate yourself for. Maybe it's the one that you still feel sick or numb over. Maybe those secrets are too big, and you need to start with a softer, gentler secret. No matter what secret you choose, relief is on the other side of this process. Once you take that one secret through all ten stages of the Secret-Breaking System, you can rinse and repeat with your other secrets. I promise you that it won't be as bad as going to the gynecologist or getting waxed.

So that you know I am here with you in solidarity, I am going to call out my secret action: over twenty years ago, when I was 26 and newly married, I got violent with my husband and threatened to stab him with a car key. Sounds crazy, right? I was a put-together woman kicking ass in the world, with the husband, the condo in Los Angeles, the friends, the reputation, the job, and the degree. In that moment, none of that mattered, because I felt abandoned and time-traveled to feeling like the little girl of my childhood, who'd been disregarded and who desperately wanted to feel important, included and seen. My childhood big secrets of feeling like I had no power, no choice, and wasn't worth sticking around for, were triggered bad.

The incident happened in a megachurch, with lots of people watching. I had a broken foot and was using crutches. Typically, my husband and I would sit up in the balcony with our friends but because of my crutches and the stairs not being easy to navigate, we stayed on the ground floor. After the service, my hubby went upstairs to go and say hello to everyone. Seemingly small action, right? Not for me. When he went upstairs, I felt totally abandoned. I felt like he'd left me and that I wasn't good or worthy enough to stay with. I panicked. All of the shame and embarrassment from my childhood engulfed me. I was seven again and felt like the little girl who'd stood by the window waiting for her dad to come home only to find out he wasn't. I felt not good enough to be in this megachurch with these rich people praising God and trying to make friendships that kept going wrong.

When my husband walked down the stairs, my feelings of inadequacy, abandonment, and unworthiness took over and I went into a blind rage. I charged at him and hit him with my crutch in the middle of the lobby (I did mention that this is a megachurch, right). He was embarrassed, caught off guard, and angry. He asked me what the hell my problem was. And I started yelling and cursing while he walked away. His walking away made me feel even worse and I chased him as if I had no broken foot, pushed him against the car, and, wait for it . . . threatened to stab him in the neck with my car key. Who has the power now? You don't leave me in the middle of the church like I'm nothing. You don't abandon me and choose your friends over your wife.

That's the dirty little secret that I'm known for. That's the secret that people love to hear when I speak and that I felt equal amounts of pride at being what I thought was a badass and shame for being so out of control. I couldn't talk about this secret overnight. It took time. I had to reach into the feelings behind the action and how I built a critical narrative about myself around the secret. Here's the deal with the narrative, it takes on a life of its own. The key never touched my husband's neck. I didn't break his skin or make him bleed. By the time the key was midair, I came to my senses and started crying and let go of the keys. He put me in the car. But in my mind, it was a stabbing. Thanks, critical narrator. That's part of the legend story of the secret. Because of the critical narrator, my feeling and retelling about what happened are bigger than what occurred. There was NO STABBING! But there was violence.

My critical narrator told me I was unlovable, had rage issues, and that because of that, no man would ever stick around. I didn't deserve to be a wife and to live in a nice house. At the time, I didn't know that the anger and rage were protection mechanisms covering up my fear of vulnerability and I wasn't interested in figuring that out. At that moment, all I was interested in was getting my husband to not be mad at me anymore (even though I was still so mad at him for leaving me by myself in the church). I was sure that if his feelings could be okay, I could be okay. My own internal regulating system was a mess.

Hundreds of people saw me do it. They saw the action, but I didn't care because I didn't know another way. And I certainly didn't know how to access, admit to, or share my pain. I didn't even know that I was in pain.

The root of those powerful emotions that caused me to take this secret action stemmed from childhood. What I was hiding, the bigger secret, that I felt less than, not good enough, and abandoned.

My denial was that my secret (the action/the false stabbing) wasn't that big of a deal. I blamed him for my behavior. If he wouldn't have left me, I wouldn't have exploded. It's not logical. My reaction to that moment was much bigger than his action. Today I know that it wasn't his action that I was responding to, it was the feelings of past worthlessness that came up and out of me like a force of its own.

I had a hard time plugging into how the secret had affected my life. The feelings behind our secrets are inconvenient. When we look at them the house of cards falls.

The secret on top of the secret, the part two I was keeping about the stabbing, was the critical narrative about how I felt on the inside and who it meant I was in the world because of what I had done. I affirmed that I was a scary person—unworthy of relationships and the life I had—because I had gotten violent with the man I loved. I felt so disregarded that I believed the world disregarded me and that I had to be louder, bigger, and stronger to be noticed. When you call out the secret, you start the process of becoming free. When I named what I'd done and the story my mind had created around it, a little bit of the power the secret had on me faded away. When the critical narrative began to shift, so did my life. It was a slow process, but the first stage was monumental to beginning to live secret-free. Even though at this beginning stage, my true self wasn't yet strong enough to lead, she was emerging and with her came hope.

 Because so much of your life has been spent consciously or unconsciously protecting your secrets, your false self has taken the lead.

As you work the Secret-Breaking System, your life will change. You will gain strength, purpose, and intuition as you work each step. I know it sounds like a big promise, and it is, but I'm a straight shooter. If this process can work for me, it can work for you. Walk with me and let's see where it takes you.

Let's get started, ladies. We are now going to call out your secret. Choose a journal that you love to write in and use it for the assignments in each Secret-Breaking stage. Having your secret on paper in one place will help you to organize it in such a way that it feels less scary and overwhelming. I didn't connect the stabbing action to the bigger parts of the punch of the secret until I did these ten stages. We will do the same with your secret, one stage at a time.

So that you don't feel alone, here are some other women who called out their secret action and connected it to the critical narrative and its reach:

> *Maria shoplifted a $.25 package of bubble gum when she was twelve. She did it to feel powerful. While the bubble gum and $.25 are no big deal, what developed next for her was that she had to be sneaky and not get caught to get what she wanted. This became a pattern that she played out at work, with romantic relationships, and even with her kids. She would tell "innocent" lies, equivalent to the $.25 of bubble gum, that weren't hurting anyone. But they were hurting her. They kept her living small and inauthentically. She would never come out and ask for what she wanted, which created passive-aggressive behavior. Instead, she would go behind people, tell half-truths, and get her way. She realized the secret was playing out in all areas in her life: her job, her parenting, with her spouse and friends, and especially with her parents.*

***

> *Jennifer came from a family where women were pretty, and men worked. She was told that women didn't have to be smart. She started letting boys touch her boobs before she had any, to pass her classes, get an ice cream cone, get attention, and feel pretty. As an adult, this led her to sleep*

with professors, bosses, and a car dealership salesman. Her secret isn't about sleeping around. It's about the way she feels about herself and her abilities in the world to earn money and to think for herself. She doesn't believe she can do anything on her own and that the only part of her that is good enough is her body.

***

Marilu shared her secret of watching porn. Her dad used to leave nude magazines out when she was a kid, and she would become aroused and touch herself. As an adult, it led to porn addiction and an inability to connect with men in a love relationship because she can't match up to what the women on screen are doing. Her belief that women should behave a certain way when it comes to sex has cut her off from a loving and intimate relationship.

Okay, ladies, it's time to let the cat out of the bag. It's time to call out your secret.

Calling Out Your Secret

Close your eyes for a minute and think about that one secret action. What is it for you? What is the scary monster in your closet? We are going to begin to deconstruct it and take its power away. To help you get started, I will use my secret as an example.

What is your secret action (what happened)?

I stabbed my husband in a church.

What does the critical narrator say about who you are because of the action?

You aren't worthy of your relationship. No one likes you and it's your own fault that he went upstairs. You will never have any real friends. Your husband will leave you. You are unpredictable and mean. You don't belong in a church. You aren't good enough.

What's yours? Take some time to write it all out then pause and apply empathy to your situation. As I share with you, I have tears in my eyes for the woman I once was who kept secrets and believed her false self's lies. I can feel the secret in my stomach and the ache of my heart for you, for me, and for the women still out there who haven't begun the process of becoming secret-free. I'm holding space for you to safely and completely call out your secret. Your feelings will not kill you. If you feel knocked down by your secret, it's okay. When you take Stage One of the Secret-Breaking System, you expose your false self, the You created by secrets and past conditioning. This false self is reacting to the bravery that your true self has shown by taking action and calling out the secret. The false self has protected the secret for a long time and exposure of the secret can feel uncomfortable. You also start to get a glimpse at your true self which will get clearer as you do the work. The physical and emotional sensations you might be experiencing in this stage are all part of the process of breaking down the power dynamic of your two parts. If you had no reaction, that's okay as well. Everyone processes at their own way and pace. The important thing is to be honest and kind to yourself on this journey.

As you take a deep breath and acknowledge your courage, know that you have taken the first step toward freedom. A deep bow down to your soul is in order. This kind of secret-breaking work is emotional and sacred. Now that you've called out your secret, be kind to yourself. You may want to relax and take it easy, or you may want to go out and exercise and get it out of your body. Whatever you do, don't follow the false self into backsliding and beating yourself up. Your true self is building muscles and you will meet her soon. After letting go of the secret (at least on paper) and making a connection to the secret (tear-stained paper), we need to work in Stage Two on part three of the secret's punch: the faulty wiring that got you secret-keeping in the first place.

Dirty Little Deep Dives

1. When you change your critical narrative, you change your life.

2. You are stronger than your secrets.

3. Your true self is building her muscles of strength, courage and intuition.

STAGE TWO

Unwiring Your Secret

Dating, aging, and dieting are not the problem. We can slather wrinkle cream on those lines for eternity, keep swiping right, or punish ourselves when we eat the pan of brownies, but our secrets are the true catalyst to our demise. Secret-keeping is a vicious cycle that entraps every woman, and the answer is not a shopping spree at Macy's or a bottle of wine. No, the answer is to let go of our secrets and shed the weight off our souls by unwiring and understanding their origin. The good news is that unlike wrinkle cream, when you apply the Secret-Breaking System, it works, no matter when you start.

Every secret has a cycle that begins with us taking unsavory actions to get our very basic needs met and causes us to ignore who we are and what's true for us to survive. We then carry little secrets of shame to mask the big secret. While we can't blame our childhood for our behavior, we can study it to identify how we've arrived at this exact moment that we're in. When we do, we'll find little treasure chests along the way that have set the groundwork for secret-keeping.

Contrary to what it may have looked like, I didn't try to stab my hubby because I was crazy or needed medication. What laid the foundation for much of my behavior and what lays the foundation for much of yours is the third punch of the secret: faulty wiring. We all come into the world programmed to love and be loved. Once we leave the womb, we need to be taken care of and we learn how to get our needs met based on our family system. Beliefs, ideas, and the need to fit into our family often morph into what our impression of love is. To survive life inside the system, we apply learned behaviors and perceptions about how to give and receive love, even if those behaviors and perceptions prove to be less than loving. We are shaped by our circumstances and learn to adapt. We develop an uncanny ability to create and keep secrets to navigate through life.

The good news is secrets have a cycle. And all cycles can be broken. What we'll uncover in Stage Two of the Secret-Breaking System: Unwiring Your Secret is your faulty wiring, tripwire, and belief system. We have to go back to the foundation of childhood to see how our wires got crossed in the first place and caused us to go to such great lengths to keep ourselves safe behind our long-embedded secrets.

What is faulty wiring? Think of it as a defective piece of your brain's communication system that picks up and alters signals from the outside world. When a belief is created and becomes a mismanaged need, that is your new navigation tool for survival. Life is run by a false self. When you look at the faulty messages that you believe about yourself and the world, you will begin to unravel the reasons that you create and keep secrets. Faulty wiring isn't good or bad; it just doesn't belong to your true self. Yet, it's created a reality that you believe is true and live up to in your false self. At its core, faulty wiring becomes the navigation tool you use to problem solve and chart your course in life.

You and I are going on this secret-breaking journey together and I'm committed to coming along with you on every stage of the path. As we travel, I will continue to dissect my secret in bite-size ways, so that you can follow along and plug your own secret into that stage. This way, no woman gets left behind! Secret-keeping is complex, and I want to make sure that you understand the nuances of your secrets so that you can be rid of them once and for all.

Here's how my faulty wiring came to be and what ultimately led to the reasons behind why I wanted to stab my husband.

In my family I believed there were two forms of currency; the first was intellect. To be adored and to count, you had to be smart, quick-witted, sarcastic, and unaffected by the comments of others. Whoever had the fastest comeback, won. You were superior if you were smart. And being smart, was the top of the food chain. We all wanted to be on top even if it meant, someone else had to be on the bottom.

You also had to be either conniving, frightening, or badass enough to get yourself in and out of situations in whatever way worked. All of those ways came wrapped in some sort of violence or intimidation. Our family was a pack. We felt protected by one another, and we knew that no one on the outside could touch us. We were like our own gang and in our house, protection was love.

In my family, you didn't ask for permission. You acted like you had it and moved around the world as if you did. We used our intellect, words, tone, and body language to intimidate, be powerful over, and take control of others. We didn't do a lot of behind-your-back sneaky behavior (although there was a bit of that). Our brand was more in your face, *I'm coming for you.* You knew when we were on the way and that something was going to go down. It was always an adrenaline ride that we kept putting tokens into, to ride again and again. Intimidation coupled with intellect were the tools I used to navigate and get my way in life.

My strongest weapon has always been my tongue. I've never liked using my fists or pulling hair. I'm not very good at it and I don't want to get hit. I can cut you down with quick wit or an intelligent comment that will make you feel small (thank goodness I don't behave that way anymore). My tongue has thrown as many jabs as a world champion boxer. And, it got better, smarter, and quicker each time.

Violence and intimidation were a way of being in my childhood home and a way to make it in the world. My dad's false self was bad to the bone in every way. It was his theme song and for many birthdays we gave him singing cards with the tune playing when he opened it. On the other side, his true self is kind, charming, loving, godly, and protective. Respect is one of his key values. Growing up, it was okay to be a bully to put people in check and to stay safe and untouchable. My siblings and I walked on eggshells a lot because my dad could make you want to pee your pants with a single look or word. We modeled those skills and all of us got pretty good at creating a version of these attributes that worked for us. I think it's important to note that he was never violent with any of us kids. We weren't hit and didn't need to be to stay in line.

One night when I was nine, my mom was across the street at the neighbor's house and her ex-boyfriend let himself in while my brother and I were sleeping. He came into my bedroom and stared at me. Although nothing happened, I pretended to be asleep, I was scared. When he left, I called my dad. My parents had been split up for a few years at this time. When I heard my dad pull up, I exhaled. I knew we were going to be safe.

He came in wearing his steel-toed boots and carrying a hatchet. I don't know about you ladies, but don't you just love a man with a hatchet? Nothing says *I love you* better than that. By the time he got there, the ex was gone. My internal wiring, however, had been crossed and from that day forward I had the faulty message that violence equaled love. That whatever my dad was going to do with that hatchet, was because he loved us. This has played out in all sorts of ways in my life. I have been violent. I have elicited violence in others. And every time, it has been a way to get that same feeling of protection and love that I got from my dad that night.

> *We have to go back to the foundation of childhood to see how our wires got crossed in the first place and caused us to go to such great lengths to keep ourselves safe behind our long-embedded secrets.*

My faulty wiring led to my secret-keeping belief that I was violent, mean and had to protect myself. My actions with not just my husband but other men before him, and intimidating others were due to my belief in my false self that being violent, and intimidating were the best ways to be. So, I would ultimately never get hurt.

Once I broke the vicious cycle that I didn't have to be violent to be loved, I could learn to speak to my husband in a calm, kind, and playful way. When a friend suggested that I could have interpreted his going upstairs to talk to friends in the church from a different angle, with zero intention of him abandoning me, I was baffled. Her framework of the world offered a completely different option that I could never have chosen because I didn't know it existed. And that's my guess about the actions that you've taken too. You took them because it was what was in front of you in the moment and how you were wired. Now I'm not saying that I didn't know that trying to stab my husband was wrong. Of course, I knew. What I am saying is that I was so pulled into my faulty wiring that it was okay to be violent to get control, that I could not see any other option. The secret actions we take and the secret beliefs we keep are perfect for the systems we've created.

It should give you a bit of respite to know that the breeding ground for keeping secrets wasn't completely manufactured by you, nor was your motivation for keeping secrets. Your family system called for you to behave this way. While it's good to understand how your secret-keeping behavior was born, we never get to use it as our excuse or crutch for unkind or bad behavior. The more we unwire our faulty wiring, the more our true self will take the lead.

Here are some examples of women who lived in their faulty wiring:

Angie believed that speaking up wasn't lady-like. She was raised in a home where her mother was subservient, and her dad had the final say on just about everything. Any time she spoke up, her dad would tell her she wasn't acting lady-like and that no one would marry an aggressive woman. This faulty wiring left Angie angry and stifled. Her relationships weren't working because she would never say what she really wanted for fear of being aggressive and ending up alone. Her secret was her desire to speak her truth, but she feared she would be single forever.

***

Madison slept with nearly 100 men. She grew up in a house where her mother never got married and told her that being tied down or beholden to anyone was like being a slave. The mantra growing up was that men were replaceable. This faulty wiring kept Madison from having a long-term relationship and children. Her secret was that she wanted a life partner, but she didn't want to be anyone's slave.

***

Tina's faulty wiring was that the world was a mean place. Her parents taught her that trusting others meant that she would be taken advantage of. Tina spent her life being smarter than anyone else in the room, calling people out on every minor detail so that they couldn't get one over on her, and going through every boyfriend's phone, computer, and drawers to check that what they were telling her was the truth. (Anyone relate, or is it just me?) Her need to know it all and to prove her point repeatedly got her fired, kept her from having long-lasting friendships, and made her lonely. Her secret? She would be okay not being right all time if she could be loved.

 The secret actions we take and the secret beliefs we keep are perfect for the systems we've created.

Part 1: Define Your Faulty Wiring

As you unwire your faulty wiring, think of the childhood stories and situations that have shaped you, and your behaviors that have been created as tools for survival. These tools often become the three of the one-two-three secret-keeping punch.

1. What events occurred in your life that caused faulty wiring? Example: My dad coming over with a hatchet and steel-toed boots to protect us caused violence

and protection to equal love for me. Our family using intimidation gave me the belief that it was okay to use intimidation to keep or gain control.

2. What family system did you learn and use to navigate the world? Example: Intelligence, intimidation, and control were tools I used to navigate the world.

3. What do you believe about yourself or the world because of these navigation tools? Example: I am intimidating and smart and can get what I want. The world can't get one over on me. If you try to hurt me, my family will protect me.

4. How did your faulty wiring contribute to your secret that you are taking through the 10-Stage Secret-Breaking System? *Example: My husband went upstairs, and I used intimidation and violence to try to gain back control.*

You take an important step when you begin to unwire the false self. Once you have an idea of your faulty wiring, you begin to embark on one of the most important reasons that you create secrets: your tripwires. A tripwire is a deep, long embedded emotion that is rooted in the past and caused by the faulty wiring of your false self. It's one of the main reasons that you keep and create secrets.

Have you ever heard the saying, *if it's hysterical it's historical?* It's a good way to sum up the definition of a tripwire. A tripwire is an emotion that is rooted in the past. When tripped, the emotion is so strong, it causes us to check out and leave our present set of circumstances and react to something that has happened in the past as if it were happening right now, almost always causing a big reaction that is not appropriate for the current situation.

Have you ever had anyone say that you're acting crazy? Or that your behavior is too much? If so, it's probably because your tripwire was triggered.

Tripwire emotions run the gamut in the feelings category but what they all share is their strength and power over us. My clients have experienced a range of emotions from feeling less than, to not good enough, unworthy, forgotten, devalued, disregarded, unloved, unwanted, abandoned, like they are a burden, and more. Understanding your tripwire is crucial to seeing your secret-keeping and creating patterns because at their essence is one of the biggest reasons you create secrets.

My reaction to my husband going upstairs in the church was not right-sized. I knew that intellectually and rationally. The feeling was so strong because he had unknowingly set off my tripwire emotions of abandonment and not being good enough. These emotions were not caused by my husband going upstairs. The current of the emotion traveled back to me being a little girl when my parents divorced, when I didn't always have access to my dad, when my mom was checked out and overburdened, and when my friends weren't allowed to play at my house because the police came over too often. These situations fueled my story of not being good enough, of being abandoned, and of being scared, which were all the bigger parts of my secret. On a cellular level, I took on the feelings of abandonment and not being good enough as part of my being. I wanted to feel anything but these feelings and created many secrets to make me appear good enough and a part of.

My faulty wiring taught me what to do when the tripwire was stepped on. After all, faulty wiring is our best and most trusted compass and navigation tool. I used violence and intimidation to get back into control, so that I wouldn't be abandoned and if I weren't abandoned, I could tell myself I was good enough. The pattern of my big secret was that my tripwire emotions of abandonment and not being good enough were triggered. Then, I used a violent action to gain control and could then feed my critical narrator's story about my false self being violent. How's that for another one-two-three punch?

Part 2: Defining Your Tripwire

Go back to the secret that you're working through and answer the following questions:

1. What tripwire emotion was triggered to create this secret?

2. What action did you take because of your faulty wiring?

3. List all of your tripwire emotions connected to your secret. Hint: if you get hysterical over it, it's historical and probably your trigger point.

How are you doing? Are you starting to get more clarity? Are you angry and/or sad? We get to *feelings* in Stage Three because I know, I was completely overwhelmed when I realized what I had to unravel to find my true self. It's mind-blowing, isn't it? Clarity brings freedom. As you take a deep and honest look at how you operate to survive and how your secret-keeping mechanism was designed, be gentle with yourself. This reflection is meant to be a place of deep understanding of your younger self who was doing the best she could to live within the walls of her home growing up. You are never too young or old to start the Secret-Breaking System because on the other side of your secrets is a fantastic you. To get to your true self, your faulty wiring needs to be defined in how it has shaped your world and contributed to your beliefs about you and why and how you create secrets. Don't rush this or judge yourself. Just let the truth be the truth. Think of it as an archeological expedition, you are just finding out facts about how you've become who you are. Each stage of the Secret-Breaking System will help you get closer to and finally reveal your true self.

Walking away from ideas that don't belong to us can feel confusing and even scary. Your false self has sold you on a belief system that doesn't fit the life your true self wants to lead. It's time to buck this belief system that has supported our faulty wiring! When we go against a belief that was implemented in childhood, we aren't always sure where to find our North Star. Part of us wants to let go of the old ideas about who we are, the world, what's okay and what isn't, but the other part is afraid to reveal what we think, how we feel, and who we truly are because it is outside of what we were taught. Our thoughts, fears, feelings, and truths that we keep on the inside and are unwilling to share are secrets of self. They are about who we are at our core at our most authentic state.

A belief is something that we take as being true. We hold it as fact in our belief system (or as I like to call B.S.). Beliefs about who we are can cause substantial amounts of damage and lead to further secret-keeping.

Here are some common beliefs that you could've picked up in childhood:

- We aren't an academic family.

- People like "us" will never make it to the top.

- If you have money, you're stuck up.

- If you ask questions, you're stupid.

- If you're creative, you can't make money.

- You can never be too rich or too thin.

- Take what you can get any way you can get it.

- Marrying for love is a way to get a divorce.

- Being yourself is risky. It's better to fit in.

- If you want other people to like you, agree with them.

- Don't get involved in other people's business.

- If you want something done, do it yourself because asking for help is a waste of time.

- There is no true partnership someone always wants to be on top.

- People with green eyes cast spells.

- People from the South are inbred.

- Women with too many opinions make bad wives.

- Men only marry women who can cook.

- It's great to have a career but it's better to have a tight ass.

Bucking the belief system to unwire your secret is powerful work. While I am the first to tell you that you are a regal queen, now is where you get to let go of the bravado and pretense or victim mentality and take full ownership for your life. Our beliefs are a part of the faulty wiring that navigates our course and when we let go of the beliefs that don't belong to us, we live less encumbered. Think of it like *the man keeping you down.* The man does not have to keep you down. It's your beliefs that have been keeping you down. You can challenge your beliefs.

Shannon's story is a great example of a woman who bucked her belief system:

I was raised by a Pastor whose belief system rested firmly on his interpretation of the bible. My siblings and I were taught what was right and wrong according to scripture. We assumed that people who were gay were going to hell. When we were out in public and my father would see a gay couple, he would say, "We need to pray for God to save their souls."

By the age of twenty-eight, I was already quite the sinner. I had gone through two divorces (from the same man), had a child out of wedlock, and had lived in sin. After a lot of self-discovery, I was devastated and afraid to realize that I was gay. I was in love with a woman. I fought the feelings, ignored them, ran from them, and prayed to make them go away. I loved God and knew that my being gay was greatly upsetting to Him. I avoided the woman that I felt an attraction and affection for. But I couldn't stop thinking about her.

At forty, I was now being asked to challenge an innate belief that being gay was wrong. This message was deeply programmed into my consciousness. I had to go to therapy, pray, and do a tremendous amount of internal work to finally realize that those beliefs didn't belong to me. They were BS. They were put in place by my parents, and I had grown up not giving much thought to if I believed them or not because they were just part of my family system. I felt liberated when I learned that I had never really shared these thoughts.

As you can imagine I was scared that my family would disown me. And while they aren't perfect, I love them and wanted their acceptance. For a while, I pretended that I was still straight. Then I started going to gay clubs and I didn't tell anyone. I started seeing the woman to whom I was attracted. I didn't tell my family. If it didn't work out between us, no harm would be done. And, what if I was wrong? What if my feelings toward women were just a phase?

After a year, I was in head over heels love. I had introduced my girlfriend to my kids. We were talking about moving in together. After my kids met her, I knew that I had to tell my family. I started with my sister who was happy for me and not surprised one bit. She said she'd been waiting for the day that I came out. My mom was glad that I was in love but not happy that it was with a woman. She was scared about my lifestyle and had her own beliefs about what being gay meant. Our relationship was rocky for a little while, but my mom was willing to accept me despite how she felt about my lifestyle

I finally worked up the courage to tell my dad. His reaction was exactly what I thought it would be. I got the lecture I had expected. He made severing contact with me seem like it was my choice rather than his. I could either change and continue keeping the secret that I was gay or, I could still see him. As much as his love and acceptance mattered to me, I couldn't go back to pretending. I felt more myself than I ever had.

 It's time to buck this belief system that has supported our faulty wiring!

Part 3: Bucking Your Beliefs

Keep working and using your secret as you answer the below questions:

1. What beliefs were you given by your parents and others that led to your secret? List as many as you can.

2. Circle the ones that aren't true for you and that you would like to let go of.

3. What is a more empowering belief you can employ? Hint, you don't have to believe it today, you will adopt it over time.

As women, we are conditioned when we are young to not ask about others or tell about ourselves. We aren't always given a reason that we aren't supposed to tell, we're just told not to. It's part of our wiring that starts the path to secret-creating and -keeping and shame. Precocious children will buck the belief system asking "Why?" Why can't I ask the lady if she wears a wig? Why can't I ask Grandma Jean why she smells like wine? Why can't I say that I got an F on my report card, have an eating disorder, or like girls? Our parents or caretakers have their own secrets based on shame from their beliefs and faulty wiring. They are simply passing what they know on to us. As we grow up, this leaves us feeling uncertain of the world, others, and ourselves. What is the truth and when do we tell it? When we don't have all the facts or reasons, or we can't be honest, we make up the parts that we don't know to feel safe. Think about when you miss the ending of a movie or you aren't sure of the details of an event, you fill in the gaps so that it makes sense to you. The same theory applies to keeping secrets.

I put together a sample list of common don't ask/don't tell narratives that my clients have shared over the years. You may have been given similar directives as a child that turned you into a secret keeper. Do any of these rings a gong for you? If so, you're in the right place:

- Don't share your business with others. We're private people.

- Don't tell anyone that your dad has another son.

- Don't tell your last job you were fired.

- Don't tell people that you went to Europe.

- Don't tell anyone how much your car cost.

- Don't tell anyone you wax your lip.

- Don't tell anyone that he broke up with you.

- Don't tell anyone that you don't drink.

- Don't tell anyone that you're Jewish.

- Don't tell anyone what you got on your SAT.

- Don't tell anyone you had plastic surgery.

- Don't tell anyone about your inheritance.

- Don't tell anyone you have panic attacks.

- Don't tell anyone your mother's on anti-depressants.

- And mostly, don't tell anyone what you think or feel.

I grew up in a family where asking questions was not acceptable; actually, it simply wasn't done. If you asked a question, it left you open to looking stupid, vulnerable, or annoying. You were better served taking matters in your own hands even if it meant creating a secret. As I shared earlier, in our house, intellect, wit, and sarcasm were the currencies that were rewarded; they were the payoff. My grandfather who was the patriarch of our family was a very intelligent, loving, and impatient man. I can remember one night at dinner my grandma asking him how he liked his soup. His reply, *"There are good questions and bad questions and that is just a stupid question."* Neither I nor my extended family asked a lot of questions because you never knew which category it fell in. This became the breeding ground for secrets. All of us would pretend to know the answers when we didn't have them because of the negative imprint this message left on us. We missed out on many opportunities to share information and to get deep with one another because we assumed instead of asked. We would do whatever it took to keep us out of the bad or stupid question categories.

Part 4: Forging New Patterns of Beliefs

As we continue to unravel your secret, it's important to look at beliefs that you've picked up along the way that may have contributed to secret-keeping.

1. What were you conditioned to believe about sharing and asking about personal information with others?

2. What behavior was rewarded in your family?

3. What beliefs are you willing to let go of right now?

Think about what you kept to yourself and hid from your parents about school, boys, your friends, sex, drinking, where you really were, who you were with in the car, what you really wore, where you got that lipstick, and whatever else you didn't want them to know. My guess is you didn't tell them everything, every time. Even you "good" girls (holla back), I'm betting that you told your parents pieces of the story that you wanted them to hear and left out the details that could make you look bad or get you into trouble.

We took this learned behavior and all our beliefs into our womanhood and became masters at hiding, omitting, and keeping secrets to get what we want, and to keep others happy. This behavior is both a coping and protection mechanism that women everywhere have used their entire lives.

We've told so many lies and half-truths to keep our secrets protected, that we don't remember what the truth is. We've convinced ourselves that the stories we've used to protect our secrets are based on truth. And even though they may hold a glimmer, it is so faint that it's hard to follow the line back to it. The way that you behave, think, and act reflects what you've been taught in your home, from your experiences, and from society as a whole. Your false self rules and dominates. Your true self has been suffocated in the constant onslaught of non-truths, false beliefs, and other people's versions of our lives.

Are you feeling emotional? I bet some big feelings are coming up. You may also be mad as hell and feel regretful. When you start to unwire the path to secret-keeping, and your pattern starts to reveal itself, it's natural to have big emotions. In Stage Three, Chasing the Root Feelings, you will uncover where your feelings and needs collide and why your false self continues to be the loudest voice in your life. When coupled with beliefs, feelings rule our world. They dictate our actions, they move us forward, and they keep us stuck in false self-thinking. When we take a look at our feelings we will see where we have lived in our false self instead of uncovering the vulnerability of the true self.

As you see your personal secret-keeping pattern, you will be able to begin to make new choices in the moments that honor your true self and break false living. It won't happen 100 percent of the time, but little by slowly, your wiring will right itself.

Dirty Little Deep Dives

1. Exploring your faulty wiring will help you begin to unravel your reasons for keeping secrets.

2. When we listen for what we need we can answer with our new beliefs.

3. Faulty wiring can be rewired.

4. As you make new choices, your world will open up to new paths of possibility.

STAGE THREE

Chasing the Root Feelings

While facing feelings may seem like it will be about as much fun as going to the gynecologist, we must get to the root of your faulty wiring. Women are emotional beings who can numb feelings because of their enormity, especially when it comes to the shame of a secret. We replace our real feelings with the faulty ones connected to secret-keeping. In Stage Three, Chasing the Root Feelings, we will be exposing the root feelings you chased behind your faulty wiring and tripwire emotions that brought on the action of your big secret, which is almost always connected to a root feeling that we have craved since childhood. That root feeling is so important to us that we will go to any length to get it.

As women, we've been told that we feel too much or that we are overly emotional. Our feelings become something that we feel shameful about. To remedy that, we create secrets about our feelings. We might act withdrawn or subdued and are told we're frigid or uptight. We create secrets around that too. At the end of the day, we are looking for the perfect dopamine regimen to help us feel just right. And rarely, do we find the perfect balance.

The root feelings that we chase, look for, and crave are connected to love—the first and most basic root feeling that everyone is after and has a right to have. Other root feelings are worthiness, security, belonging, safety, satisfaction, self-worth, freedom, and fun. Like a drug addict, we are willing to take almost any action to feel a root feeling. They are primal and we have been taught to take secret actions to feel those feelings if they aren't freely accessible.

When we experience feelings based on our faulty wiring, we are living in our false selves. We put an entire life of authenticity, connection, and purpose at risk under the burden of the dump truck of secrets that we've accumulated. When we try to stop creating secrets, we are confronted by the fear that our root feelings still won't ever be met. The mind finds overwhelming amounts of evidence to make the critical narrative true (not good enough, worthy enough, being a nag, fill in the blank), thus creating secrets to mask the feelings of our true self.

My critical narrator has told me that I am too intense, uncomfortable to be around, and people don't like me. In response, my false self has partnered with those negative stories and has handed me evidence of where they have seemed true. In my false self, I've shown up too abrasive, causing others to back away from me and to then keep the critical narrative that I'm too intense and uncomfortable to be around, alive. I've said I'm sorry when I'm not, to get someone else to behave in a way that my root feeling demanded in order for me to feel loved. I've lied, flirted, manipulated, and pretended all to make someone else happy, hoping that their happiness would be my happiness and that I would belong. It wasn't. All of those actions became secrets, with the critical narrative fueling my big secret, and then my faulty wiring became the primary way I operate. As you can see, chasing your root feelings in an unhealthy way will get you nowhere but in trouble with a heap load of secrets. I've let my false self lead through faulty wiring, but you can never serve your root feelings through your false self. You will always experience the opposite effect of what you're looking for. In the church, I chased the root feeling to belong through my faulty wiring and false self, and in the end, ended up alone.

If this deep dive through your faulty feelings and the discovery of your root feelings kicks up shame, anger, sadness or causes you to disassociate, pause. Pausing will help you to take a moment and regroup, breaking the knee-jerk, secret-creating cycle. By pausing, you will also be able to begin to start to live consciously and make new choices. To do that, you have to be able to take a clear look at your feelings and connect the dots first.

If you are feeling overwhelmed, you may need to go back to Stage One and begin with a smaller secret. You can take a bigger secret through the system when you see relief from the results. You've kept these secrets for so long, we are not in any rush, but ask yourself, how much more of your life do you want to be burdened by a false version of you that is not authentically who you are? Through identifying the root feelings you have been chasing, you will find a deeper understanding of self, and how your secret-keeping actions affect how you live and where you're stuck.

The root feelings I chased that day in the church of love, worthiness and belonging started way before I was married when I would go to bars with boyfriends and flirt to see if they would fight for me. Ironically, I didn't date men that fought. You know why? At my core, my true self is afraid of violence. But, because of my faulty wiring, I could only feel love if I was being protected. So, I would provoke violence to meet the needs of my root feelings. It's backward and messed up. I've done a lot of damage to myself and others by chasing these root feelings. My guess is you have too.

***When we chase feelings, our false self becomes
one of our biggest secrets.***

We become motivated by our root feelings, and this starts our quest to chase those feelings with the actions connected to our faulty wiring, at any cost because we think we can't live without them. I can remember feeling like I would die if I felt my tripwire emotion of abandonment instead of the root feelings of belonging and safety. I took a lot of negative actions to chase down my root feelings anytime a tripwire emotion was triggered.

Our false self acts out and creates situations to get our perceived needs met that will give us a taste of the root feeling so that we can feel liked, loved, valued, secure (you will fill in the blank for what it is for you). The problem is the way we've learned to get these feelings has been through the lens of faulty wiring because the false self has led the charge.

When my dad showed up in his steel-toed boots with his hatchet, I truly believed that violence equaled love—this faulty wiring that if you loved me, you would protect me became a root feeling. I also got the message that I was part of the pack, which led me to develop belonging, and protection as ways to prove that love existed. The feelings I became motivated by and chased were protection, belonging and love so that I could feel worthy and good enough (these last two were the opposite of my tripwire emotions). The way I went after getting these feelings that felt like needs, is what made me a secret keeper.

The thread of faulty wiring and motivating behavior to feel the root feelings has played out in every area of my life: friendships, career, parenting, and my romantic relationships. More importantly, it's played out in how I think about myself. Consciously or unconsciously, I am always measuring, you are always measuring, where we fit based on root feelings.

Here are how some women's secrets were connected to chasing root feelings with faulty wiring:

Kami had a hard time in friendships. She was in her forties and couldn't connect authentically with other women because when she was seven her best friend's parents decided that they couldn't play together anymore because Kami's mom was in the middle of an ugly divorce and Kami's dad would sometimes show up in the middle of the night and cause a scene that woke up the neighborhood. Her faulty wiring was that she wasn't good enough (by association with her parents' mess) and had to hide pieces of who she was to keep relationships. The feeling she chased was to feel good enough. The way that this played out in her life was that she would have one good friend at a time and pour everything into them without sharing much about herself. Inevitably, the friendships would end because she was too afraid to connect.

"With my last best friend, I walked her through cancer, a divorce, and helped her with her son who had ADHD. When she broke it off with me, I was devastated. It hurt worse than it did when I got a divorce. It took me right back to being the little girl whose best friend wasn't allowed to play with her."

***

Liz was an adrenaline junkie. She jumped out of planes, hiked the tallest peaks, swam with sharks, and slept with other people's husbands. She grew up in a household with edge walkers who were volatile. Her faulty wiring was that you had to be doing something big and dangerous in order to truly be living. The feeling she chased was being alive. Which to her meant repeatedly putting herself in dangerous situations.

"I knew something was wrong with me when my sister walked in and caught me and her husband in the act. I wanted to feel bad about it, and I do. But mostly I felt every single cell of my body tingle. I was alert. All cylinders were firing. I've never felt so alive as I did at that moment."

***

Cameron grew up being told that you could never be too rich or too thin. Her grandmother that would say this to her was a woman who lunched and spent the rest of her time drinking gin and tonic and volunteering for different non-profit organizations. Cameron loved her grandmother so much and believed that she had it all figured out when it came to what it meant to be a successful woman. Cameron's faulty wiring was the belief that you could never be too rich or too thin. The feeling she chased was power.

"Every time I would interview for a job, I would starve myself for several days to make sure that I wasn't carrying any extra water weight. When I would go out on dates with men, I would order gin and tonic and think I was glamourous. My

friends would always comment on my clothes, how great they looked, how expensive they were. They were all jealous of me because I drove the best car, carried the nicest bag, and went on world-class vacations. What they didn't know is that in exchange for my body and the lifestyle, I was dying inside. I had a terrible eating disorder and over $200K in credit card debt. Every time I charged something or stuck my finger down my throat, I thought it was a means to an end to be powerful and I could always hear my grandmother telling me that I could never be too rich or too thin."

Some women chase the feeling of security and are willing to stay in jobs and marriages because of the lifestyle it affords. Some want esteem and climb the corporate ladder rung by rung, stepping on others along the way to get what feels like prestige. Some want love. They give away pieces of themselves and stay in unhealthy relationships for the payoff of not being alone. Whatever the root feeling is that you are chasing, there's a reason. Pull on the yarn ball; see where it started. Honor it. Through the system, you will learn a better way to create and receive the root feeling if it is in fact the feeling that adds to your true self.

Consciously or unconsciously, you are always measuring, where you fit based on the root feeling.

Part 1: Defining Your Root Feeling

To keep unraveling your secret so that we can continue to find more of your true self, we need to explore the root feeling at the center.

1. What is the root feeling that you craved the most while creating your secret? *Example: love, protection, belonging.*

2. What's the story your false self tells you about the root feeling? Your faulty wiring may give you some clues. Example: To be loved, I need to be protected. If I am not being protected, I am not really being loved.

3. What faulty wiring moments are embedded in your root feelings? Example: dad wearing steel-toed boots and carrying a hatchet.

4. What tripwire emotions show up when you feel let down by the chase? Example: abandonment, feeling unworthy.

Every time you chase a feeling there is a cost and a payoff. Who doesn't want a payoff, right? A payoff for the life we've lived, the hardships we've endured, and the secrets that we've kept. Sadly, the actions we take to get there always cost us because the payoff is never real. The root feeling is not adequately met, and we've taken damaging secret actions that cost us in the long run. The payoff of chasing our feelings always comes in some kind of self-protection and while that sounds good, we all want to be protected, it often keeps us isolated and alone and is the very opposite of what we are searching for. When I behaved in violent or intimidating ways, I could keep people from getting close to me. If they weren't close, then I wouldn't have to be authentic, and they would have no way of finding out that I felt less than or the stories my false self told me about me. This form of self-protection kept me safe and lonely. The payoff was that I wouldn't get found out, have to be vulnerable, or have anyone know the truth about my violence and less than feelings. The cost was that I wouldn't have friends, deep relationships, or be brave enough to truly be known.

When it comes to secret-keeping, the payoffs are actually consequences. Yup. Sorry to break it to you. I can't tell you about any positive payoff from a secret that is developed by the false self. Procrastination, not having to make a decision, letting someone else take the blame, being bossy to keep people from getting too close so that you won't get hurt, being late or self-sabotaging a relationship so that it will hurt now instead of later—those are also "payoffs."

When my youngest son was in pre-school he wanted to be a part of a talent show and was going to tell jokes as one of the planets who was orbiting around in space. There were at least six other kids in the group. And for me, to have to try to fit in with all of their moms was a hurdle in and of itself because I rarely used to feel good enough, especially when comparing myself to a group of moms.

A flurry of emails went back and forth about costumes and lines and choreography. The alpha mom in charge insisted that we all make paper mache costumes. I had no idea what that meant but knew that it involved crafts and that I was out of my league. I asked her if my son could just wear an astronaut costume. Her answer was no. It wasn't in the plan.

I had a major internal freak out about the costume and told her I had no idea how to do paper mache and asked her if it was something I could just buy. She said no. We were all going to make them together and that it wasn't that hard. To me, it felt like she told me I had to go and do algebra in front of the classroom.

And then a situation developed. An hour after our phone call I got an email that she sent to one of the other moms where I was either included by mistake or passive-aggressively, saying that she had just experienced a "Gretchen Hydo" moment. I died on the inside. What the heck is a "Gretchen Hydo" moment? I was mortified. The email went to several moms. My immediate feeling was anger because that is easy for me to access. My faulty wiring had been triggered and I wanted to intimidate her. Underneath the anger, my feelings were hurt. I felt humiliated (again)! I didn't feel like I was part of the group. I had told my truth that I wasn't good with arts and crafts, had asked for a solution, and was gossiped about. I thought about what to do through my lens of faulty wiring (slash her tires, tell her to F off, get other moms to hate her, quit the school, set the school on fire, and so on) but didn't act out on it. I already had learned how to pause, and I applied it to this situation.

Instead of acting out aggresively to get her back in line so that I could get my root feeling of belonging met, I sent an email that said I was sorry that she was uncomfortable with our exchange and any others that we'd had that led her to term interactions with me as "Gretchen Hydo" moments. I asked her if she could please let me know what those were so that I could be aware in the future. I ended by asking if there was anything else I could do to make it right. This was all completely contrary to how I wanted to behave. I had started working on the Secret-Breaking System and knew that my faulty wiring was at play.

She emailed me back stating that this was "silly" and that maybe my son being in the act wasn't a good fit. I was crushed. I hated her. I had been vulnerable and exposed. An entire group of moms had heard about my "Gretchen Hydo" moment, and now my sweet son, couldn't be a part of, because of me. There is nothing like watching the consequences of your faulty wiring play out in the life of someone you love to motivate you to do things differently.

I decided that I could not use my old tools of faulty wiring to get my needs met. So, I did not cause a scene, become violent, or intimidate her. I had learned my lesson from the stabbing incident and knew that acting in my false self would no longer serve me and could ultimately hurt my son. While I compared my insides to her outsides for years and felt the despair that comes from comparison, I took new action. Here's how this played out for me, and by the way, it wasn't perfect, but it was as much as I had learned about the Secret-Breaking System at the time and the best I could do.

My faulty wiring would have me believe that it was important to be part of a pack. My secret was I didn't feel good enough so I withdrew from the group and created a completely different act for the talent show for my son and his friends where we could look better. The cost was I got secluded from the mom group and lost a community. The "payoff" was I got other moms on my side so that I could feel a false sense of superiority and protection (faulty feelings) and didn't have to put myself into other vulnerable situations. Me not having to connect made it safe for me to somehow believe that I was still good enough.

In the end, cost and payoff never balance out. The deals we create with ourselves always leave our personal accounts overdrawn. By avoiding and chasing, we're like a gambler who is always putting everything on red at the craps table, but the ball never lands on it. We lose more than our figurative money. We lose our authenticity, our truth, and pieces of our soul. No matter how hard we try to chase that root feeling down, we never really get more than a temporary high from our win and we inevitably backslide and lose more the next time we play.

 When it comes to secret-keeping, the payoffs are actually consequences.

Here are how a few women got payoffs from their secret:

Kiana's secret of never feeling good enough came from faulty wiring caused by her dad who used to tell her that she would never amount to anything. While untrue, this faulty wiring caused Kiana to let her false self lead. She repeatedly created situations where she never had to excel or work hard; she dumbed herself down and was passed over.

"Even though I knew I was qualified for different jobs, I was always secretly relieved not to take them because I didn't have to be responsible or work hard. I also never was in charge of making decisions because I told myself I would make the wrong one. This let me off the hook if things went wrong." The payoff was that she didn't have to take chances. The cost was that those chances would have moved her forward in her life, but she chose to stay small and to chase the root feeling rather than new behavior that would require her to behave differently.

*** *

As a kid, Becky was super inquisitive and asked a lot of questions. Her parents, siblings, and aunt would always tell her that she was too much.

"One time my family left me at home instead of bringing me with them to the fair because they didn't want to have to answer any of my questions. They told me they left me at home so that they could just relax and have a good time."

This created the faulty wiring that Becky was too much. The feeling she chased was that she wanted to belong and be a part of but, she was afraid that if she was around people, her "too muchness" would come out. So, she adopted a mantra that she doesn't like humans. This mantra has paid off because she gets to be alone and never has anyone think she's too much. The cost is that she's alone and that if she doesn't stop chasing the root feeling she will never know where her seemingly "too muchness" is exactly what's required.

Identifying the cost and payoff of keeping secrets will help you to continue to unravel your own personal secret-keeping system. As you do this, you will become more aware of how your basic need for safety has kept you living small and keeping secrets.

Part 2: Cost and Payoff

Think of your secret.

1. What is the payoff you get from chasing your root feeling?

2. What is the payoff that you get from keeping your secret safe?

3. What's the real cost in your life by living this way?

For many of you, if what we are uncovering in Stage Three about the MO of your false self is devastating or disappointing, take a timeout. Take space in between your knee-jerk ways of being. We want to make room for your true self to take authentic action, but it will take time.

The more you uncover, the easier it will be to catch and divert your false self before she begins to lead.

As your true self gets shinier and braver, she will show up more and your false self won't like it. You may notice your false self-behaviors getting bigger as you work this process. If it is an action that you are taking that is based on faulty wiring or a root feeling, ask yourself what you can do instead that would help you get closer to the truest version of you. It is going to feel vulnerable and nerve-wracking and it is also going to change your life.

As we continue to Stage Four, Facing Your False Self, it's time to celebrate. It's showdown time with your false self. We start to catch glimpses of the most authentic version of you, your true self. Your true self will make a powerful claim over your life from the shroud of secrets. That is the new payoff. As you begin to get to know your true self and trust her, you will take action on her behalf. Those actions might feel shaky at first and you may be uncertain as you take them. But do take them. As you do, your life will change by letting go of one secret at a time.

Dirty Little Deep Dives

1. If it's hysterical it's historical.

2. Identifying the root feeling of your secret will help you unravel your secret-keeping behavior.

3. Your secret's cost and payoff have cost you enough.

4. When your false self starts to lead, take a pause.

STAGE FOUR

Facing Your False Self

Ladies, the time has come for Stage Four: Facing Your False Self. It's time to get rid of the lies, half-truths, and distorted identity that your false self has had you hiding behind so that you can emerge as the woman you are meant to be. Powerful, strong, courageous, and 100 percent authentically you. As you've worked stages one to three in the Secret-Breaking System, you have discovered the layers and patterns that have been your breeding ground for secret-keeping. As you shed these old ways of being, your true self will stand in her own light and illuminate your path to a secret-free you.

As your false self is called out, expect her to become argumentative and loud. Her voice will be convincing and authoritative as she presents you with evidence as to why her way of life is your surefire way to live. She will remind you that the secrets you've kept are too big, too bad, and too nasty to reveal. She will continuously bring to mind how she has demonstrated friendship toward you by helping you create a pretty good life. She expects your cooperation, loyalty, and compliance in return.

Know this. She is wrong. She needs to take a backseat or better yet, get out of the car so that your true self can step into the driver's seat without a backseat driver yammering away at her at every turn (look out; there's danger up ahead; slow down!). Like an abusive relationship, you might feel unsure about making this change. You've been conditioned by your false self to believe that what's she offering is the best that you can get out of life, and that you will not find better than what she's already given to you. This makes you scared, scared to believe in hope and possibility and unconvinced that the life you're living is that bad. Dear one, don't panic. We won't throw the baby out with the bathwater. Instead, we will look at the pieces of your false self that are useful and we will honor those and see them for the underdeveloped assets they are. We don't want to hate on her for all that she has done to serve you, but we can no longer let her lead. We have to discard the parts of self that are causing us harm. The unhealthy beliefs, the faulty wiring, and the way that you chase your root feelings that egged on your secret-keeping behavior were used as your navigation tools and will be replaced by the truth. Your truth.

Like an exotic and beautiful plant, you get to daringly blossom into the woman you were born to be (cue Lady Gaga). You can finally exhale out the old and destructive ways of being that have been exhausting and damaging, and inhale in new ways that will help your true self lift her face toward the sun. We are striving to be honest, authentic humans who no longer hate ourselves, eat our shame away, or lose sleep over our secrets.

The false self has guided you to take secret actions and to hide your bigger secret about how you feel about yourself because of those actions. The same false self who had us leak confidential information about a co-worker that got them fired, key our ex-boyfriend's car after we found out he slept with our roommate (you know who you are), and steal the shirt at Macy's because it made us feel powerful and was easy to get away with. With Stages One through Three complete, the one-two-three punch of your secret has been revealed. You aren't crazy. You can stop gaslighting yourself. The reasons you created and kept secrets are powerful and unique to you, but now that you have fully faced the how and the why of your secret-keeping behavior, you can stop.

We intend to move your true self into a position where she can assure your false self that despite her best efforts, your false self has been hurt and disappointed because she is limited by her inability to lead differently. Deep down, the false self is relying on your true self to take it from here, but at this moment, she still doesn't trust that your true self is strong enough.

It's time to deconstruct the point of view of your false self, to thank her for getting you this far, and patiently make way for your true self to lead. We don't want to freak your false self out and cause an all-out rebellion. After all, she's worked so hard for you to have a life. With the Secret-Breaking System, you are guided in a way that methodically and gently shows you that you can shed your old skin and be safe. Your true self is stronger than your false self thinks, has good ideas, and can manage your life effectively. Since we're striving for balance, when you find yourself panicking or perhaps hysterical, return to the tool of pause, and reset. By pausing you allow yourself a moment to get centered, to take a breath, and to let a new idea or inspiration emerge before you come back to the work. The pause is your personal time-out and can be used to stop big feelings from inflating and going out of control. Until we put down our basket of secrets, we live as our false self, and she has created a cage to keep us in. In this cage, we settle into good enough living, and it's tricky because this kind of living can be fulfilling up to a point. It usually includes a good enough job, relationship, kids, house, money, and achievement. At its core, good enough living is missing the *more* of your true self. Good enough living is built upon safety and is risk-adverse. Good enough living stays small, intentionally, to not rock the boat because doing so would allow the secrets to spill over the edge. Your false self is a realist. She's the one that stayed up with you at night as you cried or raged over your secrets. She's been burned, betrayed, and has taken the brunt from your faulty wiring. Her persona is strong and hard to undo. So, you accept the scraps of life, convincing yourself that they aren't scraps at all. The false self's narrative is a smoke and mirrors trick, a mind game, and manipulation she uses to keep your true self in check so that you won't get hurt. This thinking stifles your purpose, creativity, and spark while it chains you to old beliefs that support your critical narrative.

Here are some examples of good enough living:

- Being the admin assistant but wanting to be the decision-maker

- Being the editor but wanting to be a writer

- Being the agent but wishing to be an actor

- Staying in a relationship but knowing it's not true love

- Having a job but hoping for a career

- Having a career but yearning for your dream

- Hiding the dream but supporting someone else's dream

- Living in the suburbs but craving the mountains (beach or city)

- Having a husband but agreeing to not have kids

- Having kids but attaching to single parenting

- Having a successful business, but not the one that excites you

- Having a master's degree, but not advancing

- Having a good life but knowing there is still something more

Your false self always keeps you a step back. You can shine, but never too much. You can accomplish, but not to your fullest. You can live but must stay under the radar. Your false self keeps you adjacent to the life your true self wants to live because she hasn't collected any evidence to prove that she can have more. Her faulty wiring has kept her so stuck in her story that she has had no other choice than to create the life that you're living today. If you think of it as a puzzle, the outside pieces are all there. It's the center, the heart of the puzzle, that isn't in place.

The reason it's missing the heart is that your false self has been created by the narrative of who she believes she is because of the secrets she's kept and crafted. She leans heavily on her scrappy tools and street smarts because she's afraid and doesn't know another way. The false self is the loudest one in the room, because your true self is vulnerable (but not in a weak way), kinder, and more intuitive. Your false self is heavy on survival skills and light on values. Your true self is heavy on the heart and what's kind and right. Your true self knows how to follow your North star and can lead to a new navigation system.

 Good enough living is missing the more of your true self.

Before my coaching career, I worked as a publicist. I had my own boutique agency and spun myself to look like I was exceptional at PR because I don't like to do anything where I am not the best. The truth was, I was good, but not phenomenal. I compared myself to other agencies who worked out of an office building, had staff, and seemingly knew what they were doing. I, on the other hand, worked from a downstairs bedroom in our home that was my office, the guest room, laundry room, and catch-all for the weird stuff that ended up in the house. I did business, I made calls, I pitched stories. I got clients placed. I got paid. What I never got was long-lasting satisfaction. Any time I thought about what else I would like to do, my false self would tell me that it was too hard, would take too much time, and not to rock the boat. It would remind me that I didn't want to be financially unstable. I was making steady money, and if I made a change, it could be risky. My false self told me that there could be devastating consequences. There wasn't anything else that I needed to go after anyway. Life was fine. But I was bored, irritable, and wanted more.

My false self kept presenting me with reasons to stay safe. You're employed, your mortgage is covered, you work from home and your kids are little, you have a great life. It's a life so many people want. You're asking for too much by wanting more.

My life could have felt like enough. But it didn't. You know why? It was just good enough living. Good enough living isn't exciting or purposeful. It covers the basics and presents itself in a better light than it deserves. I bought into good enough living and felt guilty for even considering wanting to make a change. That's the power of the false self. When your true self shows up, the false self entices, bullies, and scares you to stay in place.

By this time in my life, I had worked stages one to three in the Secret-Breaking System. My false self wasn't as strong as she used to be. The identity the false self created of me no longer felt comfortable and neither did the life I'd been living. My false self had created so many secrets to keep me in good enough living that it was hard to break free from their web. As I worked the stages here's what my true self revealed to me that I had been hiding from under layers of secrets, faulty wiring, and untrue beliefs:

- I didn't love my life.

- I was scared.

- I didn't feel like I was a great publicist.

- I felt like I had no options.

- I didn't know how to parent as well as I wanted to.

- I had people who liked me but didn't feel like I had friends.

- I wanted more than what I had but didn't know what it was.

- My marriage was in a rough spot.

- I worried that one day I might snap and be violent like I had been before.

My true self was emerging. She was showing me where my life needed work. Through her honest eyes, I saw that my false identity had created a narrative that was wrapped in my biggest secret narrative of all, the big kahuna, the belief that I wasn't good enough and would ultimately be abandoned. My life was like a tree with deep roots spreading over a wide range of ground. What I realized from stages one to three was that the life I was living and not loving was created because of the false self's critical narrative and its drive to chase root feelings. Secret actions. Secret stories. Secret beliefs. No wonder my life was only good enough.

When our beliefs and behaviors spin out of control because of our core secret created out of faulty wiring, life cannot offer us anything more than our own recycled thinking. I had no more room for another secret in my basket. I was pushing one of those double-wide shopping carts from Costco to carry around the life the false self had created for me. It didn't even have room for a pizza slice or a $.99 hotdog from the takeout window in the food court.

I turned forty and thought, is this it? This is what life is? Okay. It's all right, I guess. I thought there would be more. I thought I would feel differently. I had played my cards right, always had been responsible, had never done drugs, could count my intimate relationships on one hand, and was a "good girl." I had gone to college, had my own apartment and lived alone before I got married, bought my own car, and had the dream wedding. We owned a house, had two kids, I volunteered, I had my own business, and I had so many secrets.

Where was my fancy job at Cosmo that I had dreamed about what I was a teen? Where was the advice column I thought I'd write? Where was the book I had been destined to create? Where was my satisfaction, joy, and feeling of arrival? Most importantly, where was I? Looking back, I know that was a turning point. Wanting more was my true self's way of starting to light the path to my purpose. I just didn't know it yet.

My false self made me feel guilty for wanting more than my nice home and my family, so I didn't explore the inklings that my true self was showing me. Instead, the false self hid me behind my responsibilities, motherhood, and marriage. I straddled between good enough living and the life my true self wanted to live.

The secret you're working through the system is a product of the false self which will continue to entice more secret actions and consequently more secrets. To stop the further accumulation of secrets and cease the dominance of your false self, Stage Four of the Secret-Breaking System: Facing Your False Self will bring you to terms with the true you through the lens of the current secret.

Part 1: Living in Shadow Behavior

What is your good enough living? Seeing your life through the eyes of your true self in an honest and loving way will show you where you are standing on the sidelines of your life. Your true self is looking for the heart-shaped puzzle piece to fill in the picture and make you complete. Knowing where you've bought into your false self's narrative to keep you in good enough living will help you to see how the secret you are working through the system has become one more reason to stay small.

Take a moment to look at the different areas of your life where you want more but feel guilty, unsure, are not speaking up, or inviting in change.

Some areas could include:

- More job responsibility

- More Visibility

- Deeper intimacy

- Children/No Children

- Marriage/Divorce

- Pursuing creative talents

- Moving to live where you want to instead of where you feel like you should

- Exploring your passions

- Pursuing your dream (the book, the painting, the travel, the man, the backpacking trip, the initiative . . .)

- Wearing the wardrobe, you want

- Decorating your living space in a way that you desire

- Investing money and resources into yourself

- Taking time for you

- Self-care

 When our beliefs and behaviors spin out of control because of our core secret created out of faulty wiring, life cannot offer us anything more than our own recycled thinking.

As you start to face your false self, your secret-keeping patterns will need to be exposed so that your false self loses her power. The more you know about your patterns, the quicker you can spot them and make a new choice. From stages one to three you uncovered your root feelings, tripwires, critical narrator, and faulty wiring that all lead to taking secret actions. These actions, that turn into secret beliefs, that cover up your biggest secret of childhood conditioning and faulty wiring, are the reason the false self exists. As we unpack, explore and disentangle your pattern, your true self will step forward. What you will come to realize is that she was always there, giving you clues, you just couldn't tune into them because the false self was so strong.

It's time to delve in deeper so that you can see the inner workings of your false self through the lens of your secret all in one place. When you take a look at your secret and see the pattern, you will begin to see your false self's operating guide. As you look at your pattern, don't judge your false self. She did the best she could with what she learned. It's time for you to see it for what it is so that you can become aware before you act in the ways of the false self that will perpetuate secret-keeping behavior.

Here are some examples of secret-keeping patterns that other women have shared:

> *Cali's pattern was that she was chasing a root feeling of wanting to belong. Her mother died, drunk, behind the wheel when Cali was three. Cali's father checked out, leaving her to be raised by her grandparents. Cali's tripwire feeling of abandonment was seeded and her secret-keeping pattern was put into place. Cali's secret action was that she was promiscuous. She slept with her husband's best man because her husband worked a lot, causing Cali's tripwire feeling of abandonment to be triggered. Her faulty wiring taught her to find love wherever she could, and it almost always ended up being in the arms of a man. Her secret was complicated; first was the affair itself and second was the story she told herself that no one would ever really love her because her father had abandoned her, and she slept around. This caused her to continually create situations where she could momentarily feel like she belonged but ultimately end up being abandoned.*

***

Diana's false self had her rack up $200,000 in debt to feel good enough. When Diana was a child she lived in extreme poverty and often didn't eat for days. She wore the same clothes for years longer than she should have and always felt out of place. Her parents would tell her to take what she could get from the world and often stole from department stores and brought their winnings home. More than anything Diana wanted to feel secure and worthy. Her root feelings drove her to create an immense amount of credit card debt by buying extravagant items. One time a co-worker told her that her purse looked like it came from Ross. Diana's tripwire feeling of unworthiness was triggered and she went to Nordstrom's and tried to steal a designer bag. Her secret had many tentacles. She was a thief who got caught, had to go to jail, and had a record. The story the false self whispered to her was that the only way to be good enough was to have nice things. This kept her in a perpetual cycle of debiting and stealing.

Battling patterns is hardcore. When you look at the patterns in your behavior that creates secrets, you can get an immense amount of information about your false self. There she is, on paper. Her inner workings for you to see. As you see her, your secret will begin to make sense and so will the reasons that you stay living in your false self and good enough living. Your secret-keeping pattern can start anywhere in the cycle. It might start with the chase for the root feeling, your faulty wiring, or because your tripwire has been triggered. Whatever the activation point, all of the pieces will reveal themselves no matter the sequence of the way they play out.

Part 2: Defining Your Patterns

It's time to get the information about your one secret in front of you so that you can begin to uncover your secret creating pattern. Refer back to your answers in Chasing The Root Feeling in Stage Three.

1. What root feeling did you chase because of your secret?

2. What action did you take because of the root feeling?

3. What tripwire was set off in the creation of this secret?

4. What faulty wiring navigation tool did you use?

5. What story did you tell yourself about who you are because of the action you took on your chase for a feeling (this perpetuates the pattern).

6. What kind of good enough living have you subscribed to because of this pattern?

Take a moment and digest your pattern. You had a root feeling that you wanted, you took an action to get it, your tripwire emotion set off your quest for your root feeling, you took a bigger action based on your faulty wiring's navigation system to get the root feeling, and boom, a secret was created. What story did your false self tell you about the pattern and who you are because of the action you took? My wish for you is that through this work you receive clarity so that you can be the woman you were born and called to be. Not hiding, unsure in the shadows, but tripping fantastic in the moonlight. As you do the Face Your False Self work, you can see and understand your pattern so clearly that your false self can't help but relinquish some of her power.

So, why do we stay in our false selves? There are many reasons:

1. Life feels good enough and we've worked hard to get where we are.

2. We don't believe that there is truly more for us to accomplish that will make us feel better than we do now, or we are too scared to go after it.

3. Our good enough living has kept us safe, our secrets are protected, and we are relatively happy so, why rock the boat.

4. Our false self has created secret-keeping patterns that keep us stuck.

Patterns that happen at a subconscious level create shadow behaviors. A shadow behavior is a behavior we take based on our false self. We have done them so many times that these shadow behaviors have become a part of us. Anytime you find yourself thinking, well, that's just the way I am, you've probably partaken in one of your most comfortable shadow behaviors. Shadow behaviors are personal. They aren't one-size-fits-all. The false self is the shadow behaviors master, and the master pulls the strings of its puppet. You have been the puppet and your false self has been pulling the strings and having you behave in ways that aren't true to who you are. The good news is we can try on a different behavior at any time. To change, we first have to get serious about calling out our shadow behaviors that perpetuate our secret-keeping.

My shadow behavior connected to my secret of not being good enough kept me in constant motion. If I was busy, I looked important. When those moms at my son's school were unkind, I could act like

I didn't care by being too busy. Ultimately, being too busy kept me away from possible rejection. My critical narrative, that I'm not good enough, went hand-in-hand with my shadow behavior. If I was too busy, I didn't have time for friends. My shadow behavior rewarded me for staying busy, by not being rejected.

Different than secret actions, shadow behaviors are a piece of the way our patterns show up in the world. They may lead us to take a secret action or may stand alone. Behaviors are the way you present in the world that don't measure up to the behavior your true self would have you take. Shadow behaviors run the gamut and are individual to the person at hand.

Here is a list of the most common shadow behaviors:

- Procrastination and paralysis

- Overeating (eating all the donuts and saying they went bad)

- Lying and truth-bending

- Perfectionism

- Obsessing

- Violence

- Overly nice

- Flying off the handle

- Being over-emotional

- Detachment and lack of vulnerability

- Unable to follow through

- Checking up on others

- Bad relationships

- Overdoing and overcommitting

- Promiscuity

- Addictions

- Self-sabotage

- Negative self-talk

- People pleasing

- Argumentative

- Intimidating

- Doormat

- Self-importance

- Overdoing/over committing

- Other_____

 To change, we first have to get serious about calling out our shadow behaviors that perpetuate our secret-keeping.

Part 3: Putting It Together

Take your secret that you are running through the system and do the following:

1. From the list of shadow behaviors, circle or fill in any ways of being that you display in your false self.

2. How did the shadow behavior contribute to your secret action?

3. Write out how your shadow behavior is part of your false self's narrative.

These secret-keeping patterns and shadow behaviors keep you living on the sidelines of a more fulfilling life and have become an undercurrent of protection. Until you call them out, you're going to continue to repeat them and feed your false self. Looking at them straight on will help you transition from living at an unconscious to a conscious level. And when we become conscious, we take responsibility for who we are, the direction of our life, and step out of false self living. Shadow behaviors have become a convenient tool to push others away and from not stepping into the full importance of your life.

Here are examples of women living lives based on the false self:

Shanell was an executive producer for a big-time show. She was at the top of her game, had an assistant, a dog walker, and a matchmaker to help her find the love of her life. She could go on trips, buy what she wanted and treat her friends. She felt like she'd arrived. When she came to me, she wasn't sure if her life was all it was cracked up to be. She felt like she was chasing her tail and didn't like being too busy to walk her own dog or find her own mate. She intuitively knew that she couldn't keep living like she was but, she had no idea what needed to change and felt guilty for wanting to because everyone she knew envied her. Her false self had it all. Her true self wanted something different. Her false self made her feel guilty about that want and kept her from taking any action toward her desire to travel the world and help underprivileged youth, which was part of her true self's vision for her.

***

Jessica was nineteen when she got married. She and her husband were together five years before he died, leaving her with a six-month-old baby. She had a life insurance policy, support from her family and friends, and tremendous guilt over her husband's death because she had fantasized about him dying since the day they got married. She'd married him because he'd asked, and she was flattered and finally felt wanted. She loved him but wasn't attracted to him. In her false self, she often thought that they should have just stayed friends and she was jealous of her girlfriends who were going out to clubs and hooking up. But she never voiced how she felt. With her husband's death, she had a second chance she felt she didn't deserve. She had been trapped as a wife, paralyzed by the guilt and shame of her secret, secretly hoping he would die instead of having to get a divorce. She carried her shadow behaviors in her secret which provided a "good enough" widow life but it also kept her single. She believed that she didn't really deserve to have a partner since she had wished her first one dead, and it had come true. She stayed living in her false self fueled by guilt.

***

Monique would never make a decision. People would joke with her and say, "don't ask Monique where she wants to go for dinner unless you're willing to wait until breakfast." Monique was terrified of making the wrong choice because when she was fifteen, she got an abortion. It wasn't what she wanted to do but it's what she thought she had to do because her boyfriend said he would leave her if she didn't. She had the abortion and he left her anyway. She never told anyone what she'd done. But her fear of making the wrong decision created a pattern of inaction that kept her from promotions, relationships, and from moving to Paris to paint. Her shadow life behaviors would not allow her to live her dream.

To usher in our true self, we have to visit the past and our younger self before she was ensnared by faulty wiring and burdened with secrets. When we were kids, we had dreams of who we wanted to be. We had ideas. We had vision. We played pretend and make-believe and we could see ourselves being fashion designers, rock stars, or boss ladies. Raw, real truths were unfettered by secrets. Our true self knows something that we've forgotten about how we're meant to live. We still have those dreams and desires inherent to our true identity, but our false selves might say that they are silly and impractical. Along the path of our secrets and responsibilities, we have given up on our truest self, deciding to shoulder on because that's what the false self has demanded.

There's a story about a Buddha that needed to be moved because it was part of a Monastery that was being relocated. Upon excavation, one of the monks noticed a crack in the giant clay figure and saw golden light underneath. The monk chiseled away the clay exterior and found a statue made of solid, shimmering gold. Historians believe that the Buddha was covered in clay several hundred years earlier to protect it from being stolen in an attack.

Like the Buddha, you've been covered by your false self for protection from an attack. The protection has gone on for so long that you've forgotten the golden treasure of who you are underneath your exterior. As you begin to chisel away the false self, a shiny, beautiful you awaits. One of my favorite quotes is by Carl Jung; he says, "What did you do as a child that made the hours pass like minutes? Herein lies the key to your earthly pursuits." He's right. It's time to get out your chisel and start excavating.

Part 4: What Did You Want To Be As a Kid?

As you answer the below questions, have fun and don't let your false self edit your responses to make them sound smart or make sense. Your little girl holds clues to your mission in life.

1. What did you want to be when you grew up? When you were a kid? A teen? A young adult? Thirty?

2. What games did you used to play?

3. How did you imagine your future?

4. What parts of these answers still have energy around them today?

5. What small action can you take to usher in your younger self's knowing?

Did you feel that glimmer as you wrote down a piece of who you truly are? Run with it, ladies. Keep it close to you. Put an action around it. As our false self gains steam, our dreams dim. Life makes us feel like we aren't good enough and we agree. We get scared and scarred. We create secrets and resist leaning into who we're meant to become because we think we aren't up for what it will take to get there. Or worse, we accept that the life we have is all we will ever have, and we give up on pursuing our calling.

We live in our default future. A future that will surely exist if we don't do anything differently. Our lives, your life, my life, will not change if we swallow good enough living. To find our authentic life, we must be able to call ourselves out, wrestle with and let go of our fear and stand up to the bully of the critical narrator in our head.

This is a life-or-death situation, ladies. Your life. Your death. What do you want? Do you want to continue to live under the shadow of shame from the affair? The police being at your house when you were a kid? The mean things you say to your kids? Our greatest obstacle to moving forward is shame. That shame gives us an excuse to hate ourselves today for something that we did or didn't do in the past. We need to let that go. The shame is caused by the false self who did the best she could with what she knew. The shame erects the fortress around your secret. Under different circumstances, we may have made another choice. We get to make one now.

We can break away from the patterns we've created based on our false self that take us away from who we're supposed to be. We can change at any time. We aren't robots and we get to shift our perspective, make decisions, and make new choices. We are so used to drama creating the same reactions that were embedded from our faulty wiring that we believe there is no other way for us to be. We say things like, "That's just the way I am." It's a cop-out. It may have been the way you reacted in the past, but it doesn't mean it has to be the way that you respond to your future.

I want you to really get this. It's important. Once you see your pattern you can stop it. You have a choice to take a different action and to think a new thought.

Part 5: Seeing Clearly

1. Look at the shadow behaviors you circled in exercise three. What is your reason for using these behaviors as a go-to?

2. What's the truth about who you really are?

3. How can you use this behavior differently?

 Our greatest obstacle to moving forward is shame.

Our shadow behavior is never a one-time thing. You have to break the pattern today or the loop will repeat tomorrow. If you continue to live a life based on your false self, you will inevitably become that lower version of who you are. When you tally up all of the ways that you dim your reality, you will see that these patterns and ways of being started a long time ago. That big experience that felt like it came out of left field didn't come from nowhere. It's an outward expression of who your false self is internally and it's a good roadmap for who you will be years from now if you don't start taking actions toward your true self. Me being violent with my husband—it wasn't a one-time thing. I'd been violent in all of my love relationships, and a sibling and I had been violent with each other as kids. What we perpetuate we recreate and that includes secrets.

As you finish Stage Four, a core piece of your secret-keeping make-up has been discovered through your patterns and shadow behaviors. Underneath those patterns and the intricacy of the false self is where your true self lives. The further you get in the secret-keeping system, the louder your true self's voice will become. The more you let go of your false self, the golden Buddha of who you truly are will be revealed. To get to your golden center, you have to want to change. You won't just wake up one morning and be different, you first have to have an internal wake-up that will cause you to be different. This is where faith comes in and leads us to Stage Five of the Secret-Breaking System: Building Your Faith.

Dirty Little Deep Dives

1. Your true self can be trusted.

2. Your younger self holds the clues to your purpose and mission.

3. You can change your behavior at any time.

4. We all have a golden Buddha inside of us.

STAGE FIVE

Building Your Faith

Ladies, we're getting down to the nitty-gritty of who you really are, exposed by facing the big secret and saying no more to secret-keeping. No more lying, cheating, or stealing and that includes taking your co-worker's muffin from the break room. As you begin to see your false self, face-to-face, you will realize how valuable, on-point, and steady your true self is. Although she has not yet had the chance to lead, she wants to and is ready and capable to take the reins. No longer will you be satisfied by the life your false self has created. As you begin to build a new life, your true self, who has always been there, will guide you. But it's going to take faith. Faith in your true self and faith in a divine spiritual power who will help you to let go of your old ways of being, your patterns, and your secrets.

We are building your faith so you can come clean about your secret and put down the heavy load of all your secrets that are weighing you down.

Did I lose you at spiritual power? Yes, sister, a spiritual power. There's no way around it. Believe me, I've tried. Building your faith and having a relationship with a power that's greater than your own best thinking is the magic ingredient to helping you live a secret-free life. It's necessary and important because this power that you get to define in a way that feels right to you is going to help you strip away your false self so that you can live the life that was meant for you before you got off course with secret-keeping.

How do we bring faith into the Secret-Breaking System? In Stage Five, Building Your Faith, we look at how spirituality and religion can be a mixed bag because oftentimes we've built our faith foundation from the viewpoint of the very same people who installed our faulty wiring and caused us to chase our most basic root feelings. Their ideas about spirituality, God, and religion were passed down to us and we've inadvertently applied or rejected their thinking to this very important topic.

Through this stage, you can build faith by exploring the ideas your true self subscribes to. Your false self has been wary of faith because she only has faith in herself. We mustn't let her lead one more moment of your faith journey because the only faith she has is in her own self-preservation and that will block your path of secret-breaking.

I know it sounds like some kind of exorcism to get the false self out, and to a degree it is. We are going in deep, and we need a faith bigger than ourselves to support and love on us. Especially in the moments when we feel we can't go on with living a life without secrets. It would be a lot easier to just throw in the towel and binge on cupcakes and watch Netflix.

To untwist shame, we need faith. Big faith. This faith relationship will help us to go deeper than what's on the chaotic surface of the false self. A faith relationship is cooperative and becomes a knowing between you and this greater intelligence.

Looking at faith will lead us to the truth about who we are. What have you been faithful to? Secret-keeping for one. Faithful to holding back your real self so you won't get hurt. Faithful to co-signing other people's nonsense to meet a root feeling. With secret-keeping, we are dealing with a spiritual malady that will require partnering faith with acts of integrity, trust, and prosperity—not fear, shame, and base-level survival. There was a time, however long ago, when you had faith that people were good and the world was safe. But we've been hurt, burned, betrayed, and abandoned. We've had to learn how to protect ourselves. The faith that we once may have had might have gotten us hurt so we grew faithful to protecting ourselves at all costs. We were made to look stupid, felt helpless, enraged, and ultimately, on our own. We learned to stop trusting others and to trust ourselves because, in the end, we were the only ones who could truly protect us.

A faith relationship is cooperative and becomes a knowing between you and this greater intelligence.

As we reach the halfway point in the Secret-Breaking System, Building Faith, we have come to a pivotal moment in your journey to learning how to stop keeping and creating secrets. Remember, becoming a secret keeper was inevitable because it's part of our human condition. We've all kept secrets. With each secret we've kept, we've moved further and further away from the deep knowing of our true self and God's voice. For a lot of people, this is the place in the Secret-Breaking System where they get stuck. They might be willing to look at their secrets but are unwilling to explore faith because it's elusive and can be hard because it is something unseen. Your false self is in the protection business and deals with facts and what is, leaving faith to feel flimsy.

Having faith does not mean that you will live pain-free. What it means is that you won't have to do everything on your own because you will be partnering with a spiritual power who will help, lead, and guide you. Your trust in this power will get you through the seasons of life.

As you start to build your faith, I am going to use the word God at times to refer to a spiritual entity. Please feel free to plug into a higher power, the divine, the universe, a spirit, intuition, inner wisdom, or whatever resonates with your inner knowing so that you can relax into the idea of building a relationship with a spiritual power. This universal presence is available to everyone and there is no requirement for having a relationship. This presence is ready to meet you exactly as you are, today, and right at this moment. As we work Stage Five, you will begin to see that it's always been there and that in fact, you have never been alone.

If this is hard or feels too "woo woo," I understand. It might feel as confusing as your calculus class did. Building faith and this relationship is a process that will strengthen over time. The inklings of ideas that you have today may change as you grow your faith foundation and get curious about your definition of who God is to you. Whatever your starting point, you're in the right place.

 To untwist shame, we need faith. Big faith. This faith relationship will help us to go deeper than what's on the chaotic surface of the false self.

Here are the most common reasons people abandon, avoid, or don't have faith:

- They've been let down and/or hurt by people of faith who said they loved us or who were in positions of authority.

- They were brought up to believe certain truths about religion and spirituality and have abandoned, embraced, or found their own way that conflicts with those ideas.

- The shame of their secrets holds them back from connecting to a spiritual presence because they know that the wrongs they've done can never be forgiven. How could they be when they won't ever forgive themselves?

- They have no idea how to make a power like God attainable to them.

- They find religion hypocritical and hard-nosed.

- They put their faith in people instead of God.

- They feel like God wasn't there when they needed Him.

- They don't know how to have faith when the world is so uncertain and so many bad circumstances occur all over the world that devastate and affect so many.

- They are atheists or agnostics.

Where do you fall on this list?

Although building faith from the ground up might seem like a daunting task and relying on an unseen power might feel like the wrong answer, it's not. We have all had moments in life where something happened that was not humanly possible. Maybe it came in the form of a knowing, an angel with skin on, or a coincidence. If we pay attention, what we realize is that there has always been a power greater than ourselves in our life. We must train ourselves to see it. Whether you believe or don't believe in God or religion doesn't make finding faith less critical. Universal spiritual intelligence is there, regardless of our ability to connect, believe and plug in. This intelligence already knows what we've done and knows our path forward. Unlike our human relationships, God/ Higher power/Spirit is always on our side, always waiting for us, and always rooting us on.

For some of you, this concept may make you cringe. You bristle or roll your eyes when I mention God. Maybe you've been turned off by religion completely or you are an atheist. Maybe what you got as a kid didn't add up or maybe you didn't get anything at all. Here's what I know when it comes to changing yourself to behave with more commendable actions: you need faith. Faith needs to happen regardless of working one secret through the system or all. You need faith to let go of the false self and ultimately tell and let go of your secrets so you can lead a big life. You don't need a church or a place of worship to build this form of faith. You don't need to take on any spiritual rituals. You don't have to give up your worldly possessions or move to Africa (why is it always Africa?). Or you can do all or some of these things. Here's the truth, your version of God is with you and in you. You need faith to access it and to believe you can change no matter how that shows up for you.

At the center of every religion is the belief that there is a being higher than oneself. A source to draw wisdom and discernment from and to lean into with faith. On the other hand, to be spiritual you do not have to be religious. You can apply spirituality to your life like a warm blanket to find comfort, answers, and direction. You do not have to subscribe to any religious sect, or you may. Spirituality is all about seeking and finding your source. That source is going to help you rewire your faulty wiring and tell you the truth about who you are despite your secrets.

When I was thirteen my dad wanted me to get baptized. I had no idea what that meant and asked him if he was going to heaven. He said he was. I asked him if I was going to heaven. He said I wouldn't unless I accepted Jesus into my heart. I was floored. At the time, my dad was suffering from alcoholism and in and out of jail. I, on the other hand, was a good girl. I didn't drink, smoke, sneak out, or do anything "bad." (Now that I have teens of my own, I see that this is probably not completely true, but it's the version of me that I created back then.) I could not wrap my head around his belief that he would go to heaven, and I wouldn't. I thought God had an organizational problem that He needed to figure out. I told my dad that I was going to pass, and I didn't get baptized with my brothers. I am however a girl who likes to stack the odds in my favor. I took one of the bibles that my dad had and read the sinners' prayer so that I would be covered, just in case.

Oh, my sweet thirteen-year-old self. If only it worked that way . . .

I continued to be completely turned off by the churches that my dad took me to where the Pastor would pray for us to have enough money for the lights when the collection basket was passed. I mean, if he was the Pastor, wouldn't God get him the money for the lights? That same Pastor would ask the women to come and volunteer while assuring them they would be home in time to cook dinner for their husbands. It felt sexist and smarmy, and I never felt like the God they were talking about could help me at all, especially if He couldn't keep the lights on.

My mom on the other hand, gave us a radically different approach. She took us to Indian sweat lodge ceremonies where we would sit in a teepee (seriously) where Indians and others were chanting. It was smelly and so hot that I almost passed out. But this was one of the places my mom connected to a spiritual power, and she wanted to share that with me. She also would have us recite several Christian prayers each night. She might not have had it all figured out, but it was clear that she was searching.

Like my dad, my grandparents wanted to make sure that I was baptized. They are Catholic, and the story goes that without my parents knowing, they took me to get baptized by a Priest to save my mortal soul. These experiences became the backdrop for my spiritual path. Throughout my life, I had to figure out what worked and who God was for me. Through the Secret Breaking System, and over time, I did find a God of my understanding that I have a strong relationship with who holds me in my faith. It's not ironic that I faced my biggest secret in the house of God, getting violent with my husband, and from there started to unravel my truths. I saw it didn't even matter if my parents were right or wrong. They had offered me experiences and knowledge that worked for them at that time. What they both have given me is a gift of experiences so I could later have discernment.

These women received conflicting messages about God:

> *Mary's parents forced her to go to church on Sundays. They would fight every Friday night when her dad brought home his paycheck and then drank for most of Saturday while her mom rested in the bedroom with a headache. On Sunday they had to get up and put on their Sunday school dresses. She felt like they were hypocrites and wondered if God was too.*

***

Genavive loved God. When she was growing up, she was the weird Christian girl who would witness to people in high school. She didn't have a lot of friends because of it, but she was pretty so the boys liked her. She had always had a relationship with God, and her faith in him never wavered until one of the football players who was also a Christian got killed by a drunk driver. She never understood why that happened to him. The kids at school were angry and asked her where her God was when their friend got killed. Her answers felt hollow. Even though she had faith in God, on a deep level, she felt like some trust had been broken.

***

Cindy's mom used to tell her that God was the next good old boy who walked through the door with a Discover card. She said the man paying the bill was the head of the house. She was super confused about this for a very long time.

To start building faith so that we prevent the creation of more secrets, we are going to create an inventory similar to what you did with your secret. Understanding your ideas on faith will help you to begin to unravel your stories about spirituality and God so you can invite in new ideas that will reveal your true self.

Part 1: Understanding Your Foundation

1. Who presented the first view for you of spirituality, God, and/or religion?

2. What was that view?

3. Did it leave a positive or negative effect on your life?

4. What moments in your life have marked and shaped your spiritual path?

5. How does faith or spirituality has an impact on your life?

6. What are your current spiritual beliefs?

7. What kind of a relationship with a God of your understanding?

8. What do you believe about that relationship and spiritual entity?

9. What do you do to connect to a power greater than yourself?

We have all had experiences with a spiritual presence whether we realize it or not. It can come in many forms. For some, it's through prayers being prayed and answered. For others, they find it in the beauty of nature. While others have experiences with angels or get their answers from dreams or the stranger at the store. But we've all had something. When I was seven, I was playing at my dad's house, and I fell off the top monkey bar and got a concussion. I was taken to the hospital in an ambulance. When I regained consciousness, my grandma was standing at the end of my bed. I was crying and had thrown up on my favorite shirt, and she was comforting me. It was before cell phones, and she lived a long way away. I asked her how she knew to come, and she said it was her crystal ball. When I look back, I ask myself was this an *odd or a God* moment? For me, I know it was God.

These women felt the presence of faith:

> *Leslie was in a club with her girlfriends, and they all got up to go to the bathroom. When they got back, two guys were waiting for them with a round of drinks. Usually, they would have been happy to take the free booze. Something inside of Leslie said, don't take the drinks. Her girlfriend felt it too. They declined and later that night the guy got arrested for putting a roofie in another girl's drink.*

***

> *Angel was getting ready for the biggest interview of her career and her phone rang from her mom's old number. Her mom had passed several years before. She knew it meant that her mom was there with her for this big day.*

Part 2: Collecting Evidence

1. Where have you felt a power greater than yourself in your life?

2. What miracles have you encountered?

3. What moments in your life can you catalog and ask yourself was it odd or God?

To build faith and follow the path of the secret-breaking true you, it's important to strengthen your faith muscle and to notice the instances where *coincidences* happened or when the God of your understanding showed up. A great way to do this is to keep a daily miracle journal where you note the evidence of God's handprint on your life and the lives of others. You might not be able to see it at first but once you begin to notice, you will be encouraged by how often it's there. Odd or God experiences are a great place to start collecting evidence. Here are some ideas of what you are looking for:

1. When you feel peaceful. It could be when you get up in the morning and it's still quiet or a feeling of contentment that you have when you are in nature. It might be when you spend time with a loved one and there is a sweet moment between the two of you. Or, when someone's words touch you in a profound way. When I was working on the tripwire feeling of abandonment, my car broke down in the mountains and I was blocking traffic on a one-way road. There was no cell reception and a man jumped out to help me. He got my car to the shoulder and then jumped back in his car and yelled, "Don't worry, I'm not abandoning you. I'll be right back." That was a God moment where I knew God had not abandoned me. My car worked with no problem after that.

2. When you get the answer to something that you couldn't find out except through a God presence. There was a woman I wanted to get in touch with who I had met in passing several years before. I asked people who she was, and they had no idea who I was talking about.

When I went to sleep one night I woke up and knew that her name was Carol. It came to me in my dream. She is now the Godmother of my kids.

3. When you have deep intuition on what to do.

4. When you are in the flow.

5. When you begin to take on new behavior that there is no way you would have done before.

6. When the seemingly impossible happens.

As you begin to keep track of instances like these, you will see that a spiritual presence isn't as far off as you think. When you can start to see it in your day-to-day life, you will be able to look back at your past and see that it was with you then as well. When we have evidence, our false self lets go one piece at a time making room for our true self.

That presence has your answers. It knows your best path. It strips away the critical narrator of the false self and replaces the stories you've used to keep you safe with faith. Faith in its power. Faith that no matter what you are okay. Faith that you do not have to go back to an old way of living. Living a life of faith will take practice. The more you begin to live in faith, the richer your life will become.

Remember how I told you I was living a good enough life the year I turned forty and was doing PR? My relationship with the God of my understanding, coupled with faith, helped me change my good-enough living to a life filled with purpose. Your Higher Power is in the business of helping you shift your identity so that you can see who you are through His lens.

A few months after my fortieth birthday a woman that I mentor said to me, "You should have been a therapist." I laughed. This and being a lawyer were one of the many professions I wanted to be as a kid (other choices were a rockstar who had tattoos and wore leather pants and an editor-in-chief at *Cosmo*). This woman was right in some ways. I have a knack for knowing people. I'm the person in the elevator that when I ask how you are, you really tell me and, I help you by the fifth floor. I told my mentee that she may be right but that there was no way I was going to go back to school to become a therapist. She then said some words that changed my life. She told me, "You should be a coach." A coach? What's a coach? Is that a fake therapist? It sounded fluffy and unimportant. And I like things that are important.

But this angel with skin had struck a chord within me. My purpose chord—that chord that each one of us has, and we need to be brave and open enough to hear its chime. I had been invited into a spiritual partnership I could not ignore. I went out and researched what a coach was. I found out it wasn't fluffy at all. Coaching was about helping people who were doing okay, good even, step out of their false selves and into bigger containers of possibility. The work was tangible, powerful, and courageous. It included accountability, deep internal work, follow-through, self-discovery, and tons of bravery.

I knew that I wanted to go for it. I still had blocks and old ideas that were holding me back. My false self would still remind me that I was mean and used to be violent, this was an old, recycled story used to keep me safe that I didn't need anymore. I leaned into my God who replaced it with the knowledge that I was kind, compassionate, and a safe place. My God helped me to be brave enough to live in a new way that didn't involve me keeping secret stories about who I thought I was. Instead, my God told me who I was. My mustard seed of faith, I began to believe that my God might be right. This gave me the fortitude to allow my true self to lead. All sorts of wonderful things started to happen as I collected evidence that my true self was on the right track.

Another aspect of my false self that had told me I wasn't good enough and certainly not creative, began to slip away. I had intuitive hits that I was supposed to paint, make wreaths, bake and write. I ignored them for a while because seriously, what does making wreaths have to do with anything, but when I finally just said okay and started to create, my little Gretchen was so happy. I realized that creativity was one of the superpowers of my true self. Another thing that happened is that I got an expensive coach; this is important to share because I had money stories about scarcity that needed to be removed. This coach helped me with humility and money blocks and to see my bigger vision. I saw it and got scared and then excited and then scared. But I kept going.

The more I said yes to God's vision of who I was the more myself I became. I felt less burdened, more authentic, and like I was firing on all cylinders. I was alive. You can be too. That is why this faith work is so important. We've believed the limited view of the false self for so long that our true self has gone dim. A power greater than us can shine a light that's so bright we won't be able to see anything but our most beautiful and true nature. That's where the fun starts.

When I said yes to my God's purpose for my life, I went on a quest to learn all I could about coaching so that I could not just be good at it like I was with PR, but so that it could be a part of me. I became a Master Certified coach in record time. I felt proud of that, especially because there were less than 1100 of us worldwide at the time. It was a huge accomplishment. More than that, the work I did with others to help them step into their true self, was exactly what my God would have me do.

 The more you begin to live in faith, the richer your life will become.

Part 3: Clues to Your True Self

As we get to know our true selves, clues to our mission in life emerge. It's important to consider them even if they feel big and overreaching.

1. What inklings do you have about your purpose that you would like to explore even if you aren't quite ready to pack your bags?

2. What small action can you take to begin to explore this purpose?

3. What have your angels with skin on encouraged you to do along your path?

When we step into faith, our old ways of being become the past. A new and bigger frame of who we are is revealed and we get to carry out our special purpose.

No matter what you do or don't believe, faith is something that can be built. The way you feel about the God of your understanding today can evolve and will as you decide to give the concept time and attention. Dependence on something greater than your own thinking will create independence and assurance in yourself that you can count on. The deeper we go in our relationship with spirituality, the deeper we can see into who we are. Having a spiritual relationship is an intimate and healing gift that can reveal our truest and most beautiful nature and inner being. This revelation only happens outside of our own limited thinking. God's thinking is so much bigger than ours. What God sees in us is so much greater than what we see in ourselves. God's solutions are what ultimately heal us from the shame of our secrets. He has a different solution for each of us.

For those of you who have been hurt by religious doctrine and the humans who preach it, I encourage you to define a spiritual entity for yourself so that you have a power to lean on other than you as you push out of your default life and into the life of your dreams. One of the most powerful parts of any twelve-step program is the freedom to define a God of your own understanding. Your God can be whatever you want. You can start with a meaning that's comfortable to you.

I know I'm dropping a lot of God bombs. If you are uncomfortable with God but like what I'm dishing out, use one of these acronyms to get you through this system.

Possible Acronyms for God

- Good orderly direction

- Grand order of design

- Great outdoors

- Good old dad

- Grow or die

- Giver of data

- Get out of doubt

- Get out of debt

- Gift of desperation

- Gifts offered daily

- Get out of depression

- Give ourselves dignity

I love this last one. Will you allow yourself the gift of dignity and at least do some God exploration?

One of the most confusing pieces about having a relationship with the God of our understanding is that we come at it like other relationships in our life. We are checking God out, wondering what He might be thinking about us, and we apply our false identities to the way we interact with Him. We might try to hide who we are or tell a bit of our truth while holding back the real stuff because we're afraid it will be used against us. We also get scared that if God really knew about what we did, if we admitted it to Him then He would hate us, shame us, condemn us and confirm our worst fears that we are in fact unlovable and bad.

We also have a way of making God into our parental figure or another person of authority in our life. If your faith has been shattered by disappointing people, it's time to let that disappointment go and put your faith in something bigger. Once you do that you will be able to finally rid yourself of your false ways of being and let go of your secret-keeping behavior.

When I was figuring out my own relationship with God, I had a life-changing "aha" moment. God and I had been good for years and I knew Him and He knew me and then one day when I was doing some spiritual work, He revealed to me that He wasn't an alcoholic. Now to most people, this seems like common sense. But it blew my mind. What I realized is that I had taken qualities from both my mom and dad and defined God through that lens. Nearly every important grown-up in my life had struggled with alcohol. Because of that, I was used to walking on eggshells, having the carpet ripped out from under me, and living in unpredictable circumstances. To have the spiritual awakening that God wasn't an alcoholic changed everything about my relationship with Him. I trusted Him more. I revealed more of myself. He revealed more to me about me and about Him as I leaned into the relationship. Knowing that he wasn't an alcoholic let me settle in.

We get mixed up in our definition of who God is and how He acts because we sometimes give him human attributes from people in our life that we have trusted who have hurt or confused us. This keeps us from having a solid relationship because we stay just out of arms' reach for protection. For a lot of us, we've made our parents into our first higher power, and the characteristics that they possess we've attributed to how we understand and interact with God. Sometimes this happens with our pastors or rabbis or any people of spiritual significance that have absolutely nothing to do with God, but we unconsciously group them in our God bucket and stop trusting.

These women struggled with their image of God:

I did not want anything to do with God because every time I tried to pray, I thought of the Sunday school teacher who molested me and told me not to tell. If God truly cared about me, why would He let that happen?

***

God was not someone I trusted because my dad would hit my mom and she prayed to God every day. I didn't understand why he would ignore her and assumed if I bothered to pray, He would ignore me too.

***

The night my boyfriend dumped me I ran home and cried to my dad. We were a praying family and I asked him if we should pray. He told me I was a silly girl and that those weren't the kind of things to bother God with. So, I didn't bother God with anything.

That voice that's telling you that your secret is too big and that God will not forgive you is wrong. The limited way that others interact with God doesn't have to define Your God story. We put faith in the wrong areas and make other people our God. We make money God. We make achieving God. We make our lovers God. None of it will fill you up the way Your God will. However, you've been turned off by Your God, it's time to turn back on. You might have some resentments that you need to air out before you can start the relationship. There may be some questions that you need to ask of Your God before taking a step forward. I understand that. Your God wants to hear it.

 Higher Power is in the business of helping you shift your identity so that you can see who you are through His lens.

I've shared with you my story on spirituality and religion. I told you about my dad wanting me to get baptized to make sure that I go to heaven and my mom taking me to the sweat lodges, and my grandparents secretly getting me baptized when I was a baby to make sure that no matter what my parents did or didn't teach me about God, my soul would be okay for eternity.

What they all knew was that I was going to need a spiritual connection with something greater than myself to make it in this life.

They knew the world is rough and that things happen, and we need something outside of our own best thinking to guide us. For all that they knew and shared with me, I still had to figure it out for myself.

No human power can relieve you of our secrets. Not your therapist, best friend, mother, dad, or spouse. Even if you tell, you need to have faith for the system to work. You have to plug your umbilical cord into Your God to tell you who you are and to shed your false self and rid yourself of secret-keeping behavior. As you do that, you will be ready for Step Six: Preparing to Tell Your Secret. There is no doubt that you will want to partner with Your God for that! Ladies, I commend you for taking a look at your faith or lack thereof. You are not a hopeless case. Building a faith foundation is a key to living a joyful life full of satisfaction and purpose and as you evolve, so will your understanding and relationship with Your God. You don't have to get it all at once, in fact, you won't. What's important is that you start.

Dirty Little Deep Dives

1. Your God has always been with you.

2. Your faith will carry you through breaking your secrets.

3. God is personal and not one-size-fits-all.

4. God will help you with your dirty little secrets.

STAGE SIX

Preparing to tell your Secret

It's time for a feeling check. How are you doing? You've uncovered a lot of truth bombs about who you are and who you aren't and are just beginning to emerge into this new way of life. You now have a stronger handle on faith, and you would like to leave your false self in the rearview mirror. Like waking up after a long night out, you are coming to, in mind and body. Be gentle with yourself and be nice to you as you continue down this path. This work isn't for the faint of heart and you're still here, doing it. Although the temptation from the false self to sabotage your progress might be there, please don't spend a lot of time judging yourself and wondering if you're doing it right or doing enough. Starting and doing each step to the best of your ability is all that's important. As you rinse and repeat the system with your other secrets, you will go deeper and continue to unlock the hidden doors of your heart. We can't get it all at once. It's simply not possible. Bit by bit, we do become free as a new understanding about our true selves sets us on solid ground.

We are now at Stage Six of the Secret-Breaking System: Preparing to Tell Your Secret. Before you panic, take a breath and get centered.

You've already called out your secret, uncovered its creation, faced your feelings, revealed and reflected on your patterns and shadow behaviors, and cracked the door to building faith. As much as you may have resisted getting this far, you're here and you can do this too. One step at a time, left, right, left, you will let go of your shame so that you can triumphantly hold your head up high in all areas of your life.

Thoroughly looking at your secret and its tentacles might seem like it should be enough. It's not. You have to tell to be rid of the secret and its remnants and shut the door on your false self, for good.

It's necessary to see the damage your secret has caused you physically, mentally, and emotionally. And you will, when you tell another woman because you will be giving yourself a voice. Women have been conditioned to be silenced and we use secret-keeping to cope. Not giving voice to your secret by telling would shortchange the hard work you've already done. You would still hold bits and pieces of the shame of your secret and perpetuate the damage and secret-keeping. You're done with that. We don't want any remnants of shame lingering and tempting you with your false self's ways of being. Once you tell your secret, it is almost impossible to go backward in your behavior because you have set a new standard that is so high and integrous, it doesn't allow for backsliding. And that, ladies, is why it's time to go all in.

I know you like the idea of having a kick-ass life much more than the idea of telling your secret. Unfortunately, you can't have one without the other. Here's the good news, you've already admitted your secret and the entire truth about it, to the most important person in this equation, you. You have faced your *self* and have gone to great lengths to understand the cause of your secret-keeping behavior. Now it's time to make room for the promise of the Secret-Breaking System, which is that you will live a life secret-free.

Speaking the honest truth is a requirement to be able to live a life free of your chaotic thinking and the pain caused by secrets. Once you tell each secret, the secret-keeping action is over, and you can start rewiring your true self. Until then, your false self continues her sneaky behaviors. As unappealing as this may sound, telling is the only way to usher in a more authentic, vibrant, and powerful true self who takes actions that are decent, in integrity, and out of self-love. You speak out loud what you have held so long inside, to purge it to completion.

I know you want to be free of shame. I want that for you too. Your false self and shadow behaviors are only allowing you to experience second best in your life. The shame, lies, and regret of the past will lift as you speak the truth.

So, what is this damage that's been done? Besides living a whole life in false self, it's scientifically proven that keeping secrets hurts. Holding a secret can create anxiety, stress, depression, agitation, isolation, and worry — and can even manifest in physical symptoms like back pain, high blood pressure, insomnia, stomachaches, headaches, and more.

As a secret keeper myself, I experienced terrible colitis from the accumulation of the falsities I lived with or signed up for that almost landed me in the hospital. For a long time, neither I nor the doctors could figure out what was wrong. I hired a trauma therapist and as I told her each and every secret about who I was, what I thought, the truths I believed about myself, and what I'd done, my colitis disappeared. It was liberating to tell the truth and let it roll around the floor of her office. When the secrets were out there to be examined, my mind stopped racing. I felt better. The stories I had authored about who I was got to be rewritten. My beautiful true self showed up. I have to tell you, my true self and I have moved on to accomplish goals that I could not or would not have been brave enough to do if I were still living under the protection of my false self.

 Once you tell your secret, it is almost impossible to go backward in your behavior because you have set a new standard that is so high and integrous, it doesn't allow for backsliding.

Here are some examples from secret-keepers about how their secrets were manifesting and affecting their lives in a physical and emotional way:

Jennifer had terrible social anxiety. She would avoid seeing her friends, turn down invitations, and even started getting her groceries delivered instead of going to the store. She didn't realize it at the time, but the perpetual worry about her secrets was costing her a life of connection. She had lost nearly every friend she had. At the time, she did not correlate secret-keeping to social anxiety but, as she started doing the work and healing from her secrets her social anxiety lessened and her stress headaches went away.

***

Karen was exploding at her kids all the time. She was short-fused and ill-tempered and would react to the smallest inconveniences. By chance, she started working the Secret-Breaking System and realized that so much of her false identity was wrapped up in keeping secrets that she viewed herself as a terrible mother. She began to do the work and the relationship with her kids changed. Today she has more patience and love to give to them and herself.

***

Eileen was chronically ill. She called in sick at least once a month because of her frequent stomachaches. Many nights she would toss and turn unable to sleep. She had seen several doctors who could not find a medical answer to her condition. They treated the symptoms but couldn't find a cause. Eileen's mom recommended that she see an acupuncturist. Eileen wasn't into that sort of thing, but she was out of sick days and couldn't afford to lose her job. She went and the acupuncturist asked her what she was holding in. At that moment, she knew exactly what was making her sick: it was her secret.

Part 1: Secrets and Sickness

Circle the symptoms you've experienced from the secret you are working through the system.

- Missing work

- Avoiding social situations

- Feeling anxious, depressed, sad, shameful, fearful

- Angry explosions

- Loss of sleep

- Addictive behaviors

- Loss of appetite

- Unexplained physical ailments (headaches, stomachs, ulcers, frequently not feeling well)

- Other

Secrets don't stay in a tiny compartment locked in the bottom of your being. Instead, they affect almost every area of your life. As you begin to see how your secrets took you down, it will give you more motivation to follow through and do the work. If a secret was neat and tidy, there would be no need to work the Secret-Breaking System. You could just keep collecting secrets and store them away. But they aren't tidy. They are as insidious as weeds, that grow and suck the life out of the beautiful garden that is you.

That's why a thorough dive into the one-two-three punch is important to connect the dots with each secret. As much as your secrets can create physical ailments, they also create a psychological impact. Psychological contracts run deep and often fuel much of our secret-keeping behavior. Looking at and coming to terms with the contracts you've consciously and unfocusedly created is an important piece of preparing to tell your secret because it helps you to get a clearer view of your secret and the arrangements you've made because of it. It will also help you to organize your feelings and behaviors in a straightforward way that will make them less convoluted. The more simplified our secrets become, the easier it is to share them with others.

Every relationship you're a part of has a psychological contract associated with it. These contracts are the unwritten expectations that each person agrees to even if the agreement is never spoken. These informal obligations are developed in all relationships and become the guidelines for behavior between you and another individual. These contracts are an exchange of energy, resources, love, safety, and ways of being. I will do this and in exchange, you will do that. On the surface, they pose no problem, but when you take a deeper look at the unspoken expectations, it's no wonder that you've created secrets. As you read the following section, think about your secret and who the contract you created was with. Get it as clear as you can in your mind and heart because we're about to break it.

Psychological contracts come in all forms and at first, might be hard to identify. Once you begin to see them in one relationship, you will see them everywhere. Psychological contracts are in place when you exchange a part of yourself with someone else to help you get your root feeling met. Many times, the contract itself becomes a secret or the secret is created and kept because of faulty wiring.

Here are some examples to help you begin to uncover the psychological contract that is a part of your secret.

- An employer will look the other way when an employee uses work time to check personal email and in exchange, the employee will work late without complaining. The root feeling for the employee is security.

- A father favors his daughter over his son and in exchange whenever the mother or son says something negative to or about the father, the daughter takes his side. The root feeling for the daughter is love.

- Grandparents pay for private school for their grandchildren and in exchange, they get to choose which sports, activities, and summer camps the kids go to, regardless of what the parents want. Root feeling for the parents is feeling good enough.

- A very attractive woman commits to a not-so-attractive male and in exchange, she can take advantage of his generosity, flirt with others, and treat him unkindly. The root feeling for the woman is security.

- A rich husband keeps his wife dressed to the nines, she can have anything she wants, first-class vacations, weekends away with friends, designer everything, kitchen remodels, and more. In exchange, she won't say a thing when he's too rough with her in the bedroom and comes home drunk. The root feeling for the woman love.

These are messed up, right? Psychological contracts are the final pieces that keep the faulty wiring from being broken once and for all. We can be aware of our faulty wiring but if you don't break that psychological agreement attached to the secret nothing matters. You have done all that work for nothing! Does that upset you? It upsets me for you! You're not thinking about the agreements on a conscious level. People are not going around talking about their psychological agreements especially if they have secrets that are keeping them afloat or at the status quo. This survival tool that in the beginning felt fine because of your faulty wiring can't be in the toolbox any longer. This is the make-it-or-break-it moment, where you decide which life you want to have. Do you want door number one of good enough living or are you brave enough to open door number two and go for great? Door number two it is. Let's do this! It's time to get started identifying and breaking the psychological contract of your secret.

These ladies signed up for psychological agreements for payoffs based on their faulty wiring:

When Sarah was a kid all she wanted was to be taken care of. She was tired of being poor and seeing how her mom was treated by low-class men who drank, slapped her ass, and womanized her. When she married the doctor, her dreams came true. She would never have to worry about money. Her root feelings of safety and love were being met but in a faulty way. A few months into their married relationship her husband started asking her to dress up like a prostitute when they had sex. In the beginning, she thought it was harmless enough. Over the years, it escalated to him having her wait on street corners dressed in trashy clothes, where he would pick her up and then engage in dirty sexual acts in the car. Their psychological agreement was that he would take care of her financially and make her feel secure, and loved and in exchange, she would degrade herself sexually. She did not want to live this way anymore but still wanted the security.

***

Donna was a driven, A-type woman who wanted to climb to the top and earn her doctorate. During the middle of her school term, her mother got sick, and she fell behind. Her professor took a special notice of her and gave her extra time. It started friendly enough and then led to them sleeping together. The psychological agreement was that she would sleep with him, and he would help her get her doctorate. She wanted to earn her doctorate in her own right but was afraid that she would always be tarnished because of what she'd done in a weak moment.

***

Melissa's mother was insecure and treated Melissa like a friend instead of a daughter. Melissa knew far more than she should about her mother but never thought anything of

111

it. Her mom would often tell her that she was glad they had each other because you couldn't depend on a man. Whenever Melissa would start to date, her mother would inevitably have some drama that would pull Melissa's attention away from the new relationship causing each boyfriend she had to break up with her. Her mother would always console her and reassure her that she would never leave her. The psychological agreement was that Melissa would be there for her mom at a cost to having a partner and in return, her mother would never leave her, and Melissa wouldn't be abandoned. This filled Melissa's root feeling of belonging. Melissa worried that if she told her mom the truth, that she wanted a relationship, she would lose her mother's love.

Every relationship you're a part of has a psychological contract associated with it. These contracts are the unwritten expectations that each person agrees to even if it the agreement was never spoken.

Part 2: Facing Your Psychological Contracts

Answer these questions about your current psychological agreement attached to your one secret:

1. Who is the psychological contract with?

2. What is the contract/exchange? I will get this and in exchange, you will get that.

3. How did this contract lead to your secret?

4. How old were you when you made the contract?

5. How do you feel about the contract today?

6. What are you sad, angry, hurt, and scared of because of this contract?

7. What are you grateful that this contract taught you?

8. How would you like to change this contract? Would you like to cancel it? Make it null and void? Or revise it? If so, how would you like to revise it?

9. Take these prompts and put them in letter form and start with the prompt: As of today, I am changing the contract between me and (fill in the blank). The initial contract that . . . is now null and void. The new agreement is . . . (Credit: @FernGorin of The Life Purpose Institute)

Do not physically give the agreement to anyone. This is a step for you to process and to prepare so that you can begin to get ready to tell your secrets without being ensnared in the agreement.

Examples

As of today, I am changing the contract between myself and my husband that I will behave like a prostitute to receive your love. Our agreement is null and void. The new agreement is that I will respect myself and am willing to earn my own money while having a healthy sexual relationship with you.

***

As of today, I am changing the agreement between myself and my professor that I will sleep with you to get a doctorate. Our agreement is null and void. The new agreement is that I will ask for help as needed while keeping my clothes on.

***

As of today, I am changing the agreement between myself and my mother that I will act as your best friend at the expense of having a partner. Our agreement is null and void. The new agreement is that I will have healthy boundaries with you and a loving relationship.

When you take a stand to break these contracts, you are no longer sacrificing yourself and your life by keeping the secrets entangled in these arrangements. You are no longer giving yourself less to give another more at the detriment of your spiritual, physical, and emotional well-being - that's good news!

Now that you've been brave enough to look at your psychological contracts and access the damage your secret has done to your life physically and emotionally, it's time to risk assess. A Risk Assessment is a way to get all your fears out on paper of what could happen when you tell your secret. Once you can play your worst-case scenario all the way through, it will be less scary.

I know this work seems relentless (because it is) and is full of truth serum that once you know, you can't ignore. It might feel uncomfortable to come to terms with how your secrets have hurt you and the agreements you've made that set them up for success, but now that you know you do not have to spend another minute living this way.

Bravery is required in this stage so that you can look inward in a way that will ultimately open the door to you moving forward. Boldness, empathy, honesty, and goodwill toward self are a requirement for taking a thorough and compassionate inventory of your secret. You may be thinking, I am not feeling so brave. I am more like a coward. Look at me hiding behind all this shame and pain. You may be surprised by all the times you took a step forward, made a stand, or spoke up for yourself. The real you is waiting to reveal herself and we are going to find her.

Here are some secrets that women were scared to tell because the consequences felt so high.

My child was never "student of the month." Not once. Never. I wanted one of those stupid bumper stickers so bad that I stole one from the school office and put it on my car. He would always ask me who it was for. I would tell him it was for him. But it was for me. I deserved it for all of the homework and projects that we and by we, I mean I, did to get him through school. I felt like I could never tell this secret because I would look like a horrible mother.

***

I was arguing with a guy I was dating, and he wanted me to leave his house, but I refused. I ran up the stairs and he chased me. I grabbed a skateboard and hit him in the face where it busted open his eye and I left him there bleeding instead of taking him to the hospital. I found out later he had to get tons of stitches. I knew I wouldn't get in trouble because a lot of men are too ashamed to admit that they are getting beat up by a woman. I've been physically abusive with many of my partners to the point that if I were a man, I would have been locked up by now. I used to rationalize it by saying that I'm a woman, so it doesn't really count. It does though. I was afraid to tell for a few reasons: 1. I didn't want to go to jail, 2. I didn't want to be looked at as crazy or violent, 3. I didn't want my new boyfriend to break up with me, and 4. I didn't want to take financial responsibility for the medical bills.

***

I never learned how to protect my body. I have been pregnant a total of eight times, however, only have three living children. I was never promiscuous at all; however, with each boyfriend, I failed to follow through with proper birth control. At sixteen years of age, I mentally and partially physically willed a miscarriage. At age twenty-one, I underwent a drug-induced abortion. And at twenty-four, I suffered an ectopic pregnancy which, after surgery to remove my fallopian tube, left me in the hospital for a week. My last miscarriage happened after all three of my children were born. If anyone knows this about me, they will think I am a terrible human who has killed so many babies. My kids will look at me like a monster and my husband will think I am irresponsible and selfish.

***

When I was around ten, I did something that makes my stomach churn. I was in early puberty and my body was starting to respond with pleasure to physical touch. I was away for the summer, spending some time at a summer cabin that we shared with other members of my family. My three years younger cousin was the only girl cousin I had anywhere near our age, and we would always play in the summers at that summer home. One day, we decided to play in a smaller cabin, about one hundred yards removed from the main house. In that game, I would lie on a bed in the cabin with my undies either down or slightly pushed to the side. She would come into the room, and she would touch me around my vulva. Then she would leave the room and return and repeat the same thing several times. I was asking her to do it because it felt really good. I'm afraid that if I tell, someone will press charges against me and that I will be labeled as a sexual deviant or even worse, a child molester.

Part 3: Taking a Risk Assessment

1. What is your biggest fear about telling your secret?

2. What is it costing you to keep your secret?

3. What will you miss out on if you continue to live the way you're living?

4. Are you protecting anyone with your secret? You? Someone else (name who)?

5. What are you imagining would happen to them if you told them?

6. What are you imagining would happen to you if you told?

7. On a scale of 1–10 how likely is it that these imagined consequences will occur?

8. If these situations or scenarios did happen, how would you take care of yourself?

Right-sizing our thinking about the consequences of our secret will make it easier to move forward and tell it. The disastrous thinking that our false self has created is just another aspect to notice. The story of what will happen if you tell, may or may not be true and you won't know the fallout, if any, until you do it. This work is like facing the boogie man under the bed. When you shine the flashlight on him, you can prepare for the worst, but more often than not, the boogie man isn't waiting for you. It's just your mind playing tricks on you one more time.

There is one more step you need to do to prepare yourself to tell the secret. We are going to recap the secret in its entirety with our secret-keeping template so you have a succinct plan of telling. This is key to the preparing process—looking at all sides of the secret before you let the cat out of the bag. You don't want to just download for hours on someone a disjointed hysterical mess of confessions. The system is organized! You can test out the process with your one secret first and then rinse and repeat for the others. The Secret-Breaking System is here for you for life!

Preparing to Tell Your Secret Template

- Secret action: I had unprotected sex which led to me putting a baby up for adoption.

- Critical narrative: I am irresponsible and unworthy of being a mother.

- Big secret: I put the baby up for adoption because if I didn't my dad would disown me because I would be an embarrassment and unlovable.

- Ailment: Mental illness/anxiety/eating disorder.

- Who the psychological contract is with: My dad because he didn't ask, and I didn't tell (even though he knew).

- Consequences: A child I gave up for adoption I have never seen.

- Risk assessment: Shatters a wholesome image, endangers the relationship with dad, causes problems with parents and current husband and children. Possible consequences for child I gave up.

- Who I harmed: Myself, the baby.

You can run your secret through this template before telling. Here is the good news. You will not have to share it with people you don't feel safe with. Telling one person is all that's required. Making the risks so much lower than you think, and the benefits are so much higher than you can imagine.

 The boogie man isn't waiting for you. It's just your mind playing tricks on you one more time.

Special note, now that you've decided to go all-in, as tempting as it may be, this is not the time to run out and apologize to everyone you have hurt and to tell them the deepest details of your secret. Reframe from calling your ex to have a meaningful conversation or coming clean with your boss, your husband, or your best friend. We need to take care with how we tell our secrets. I know this from experience. As I was breaking free from secret-keeping behavior I thought it would be a great idea to get in touch with my ex and tell him how sorry I was for the wrongs I had committed against him (and there were a lot). The problem was I was engaged and when I went to tell my ex the truth, I ended up creating another secret and having what I like to call, an overlapping relationship (cheater cheater). So, let's put the brakes on the actual telling of your secret until we get to Stage Seven where I lay out the process of how, when, and to whom you share your truth. Right now, at this moment, I want you to give a big *hell ya* to the emotional, physical, and psychological damage your secrets will no longer cause you. Girl, shake the false self off! Are you ready to take the next stage? Let's go.

Dirty Little Deep Dives

1. You can live a kick-ass life.

2. Letting go of good enough makes way for great.

3. It's time to cancel your psychological agreements.

STAGE SEVEN

Tell Your Secret

Ladies, we've arrived at Stage Seven in the Secret-Breaking System: Tell Your Secret. Here you will sit another person down and reveal the one-two-three punch of your secret. When you do, you will finally, experience the full relief that comes after shedding the secret once and for all. For those of you who are still on the fence about telling, read this stage, follow the suggestions and then just do it. Get into action and let the telling begin! You've been prepared through the work in Stages One through Six. You will live through the discomfort of your anxiousness about telling because of the simplicity of the template, your awareness of the psychological contracts, and your desire for a life that is full of purpose and minus secrets. The moments leading up to the telling can be nerve-wracking but the moments right after are often elating. Keeping your secret any longer is not one of your options. It's time to let the final stages of the shame go.

Okay, I'll tell. But who? Here's the scoop on the lucky person you choose. They must be someone you feel safe enough with to bear from your soul, the secret that has been locked away deep inside you and silenced, for all these years. Consider choosing someone who is nonjudgmental, trustworthy, and discreet. You are not looking for someone to be on your "side" because there is no side in secret-keeping. The person you choose may be able to create new awareness for you around your secret, so look for wise people in your circle. Also, no dropping bombs on naïve listeners. Telling the lady at the Yarn Barn about you stole money from your employer may not land so well, no matter how motherly she has been to you. You are looking for someone who can create a safe space for you to be completely honest so that you can move forward and embrace your true self.

As you work through the system again in the future (because once you get rid of one secret, you want them all gone!), you may decide to share different secrets with different people for a variety of reasons. Some people choose to tell a therapist or person of faith a really personal secret that could be detrimental if exposed. Some people start with a third party and use it as a dress rehearsal to tell someone who is a more intimate part of their life. You could rely on a coach or mentor for a different kind of secret perhaps with how you have done business or financial issues. Some secrets work well with a trusted friend or advisor.

As you figure out who the safest person is to reveal yourself to, remember that you are in a vulnerable place right now. While ultimately getting rid of the secret is paramount to your better life and health, this is not the time to drink a bottle of wine and confess to your ex all the cheating you did while you were together. Don't tell a co-worker you barely know in the break room about the abortion you had. When the grocery clerk asks you how you are, do not reveal that you've given seven people herpes. Although you may be tempted to start revealing your secret to just about anyone because you're spilling over from its weight, use mindfulness. The key to being successful with this stage is to consciously choose the person or people you are going to trust and reveal your ONE secret to.

As much as you need to feel safe, you must consider your audience and weigh the consequences of what it will mean to them, to hear your secret. Reflect on how your secret might affect that person in a negative way. Let me break it down. If you're good friends with your husband's sister but you cheated on your husband, pick someone else to tell. Perhaps telling your secret to the person you would like to share it with will open old wounds or create new drama for them, take them off your list and choose a different person. The point in sharing your secret is never to hurt someone else or yourself. It's to come clean about the secret you've been hiding and to reveal those truths so you can stop the patterns of the false self . . . and stop creating more secrets!

Coming clean with your secret is not a directive given to punish you or to make you feel worse about yourself. This stage was designed to get rid of the handcuffs of shame so that you can empower yourself to live without secrets overall moving forward in a faith-driven life of your truest self. In Stage Eight, we will dive into how to live a secret-free life. Until then, the only action in front of you is to find someone who you can trust to speak your secret to.

Part 1: Identifying Who to Tell Check List

Choose someone who:

- Will not be put into an awkward position or harmed by learning your secret.

- You trust to hold this information as private and while keeping you in their highest regard.

- Will not try to fix or save you but instead will listen objectively and compassionately.

- May have wisdom they can share with you.

- You trust.

- Your intuition is leading you toward.

- You have no attraction or sexual charge with. It is especially important not to tempt yourself with physical or emotional comfort from this person. It will distract you from the work and possibly end with more secrets.

After considering who to tell, write down three possible people to share your secret with.

Special note: Be aware this is a vulnerable business and who you tell may suddenly look like potential love material. Remember, as good as it might feel to finally be vulnerable, the secret receiver is simply holding space for you. Your root feeling may be activated because of this connection and the intimacy that can show up with your telling. This kind of radical acceptance can feel like love, belonging, and safety. I can't tell you how many rational women have made this mistake. Secret telling is potent. Be warned, this is not the time for celebratory sex with this person or to start fantasizing about engagement rings. This is a no-no to ensuring that this Stage works and so that you do not inadvertently create a new secret. Be on guard, tell your secret, and go. Thank you very much.

Now that you've identified who to tell, let's talk about what to tell and how. This is important because there is no need to overshare. You want to keep it simple, truthful, and complete. Using the "Secret Template" from Stage Six will help you to be direct without getting lost in the details. It's best if this process is done face-to-face, human-to-human, instead of over your device. Making eye contact, sharing a hug, and seeing a smile or a nod of recognition are part of the healing in this stage.

The point in sharing your secret is never to hurt someone else or yourself. It's to come clean about the secret you've been hiding and to reveal those truths so you can stop the patterns of the false self . . . and stop creating more secrets!

When you choose who you are going to tell, let them know that you have been working through the Secret-Breaking System and you need their undivided attention to get a long-held secret off your chest. Are they prepared and willing to hold space for you? Imagine if you started to tell someone your darkest secret while they were picking their kids up from preschool and had you on speakerphone? They may be more than a little caught off guard. You don't want to drop a bomb and just blurt it out either. Remember, this is a thoughtful, prepared process that will bring you great healing. It shouldn't be done in a rush or on the fly. You want it to be complete and completeness requires space and time. Pick someone who can give you that space.

Invite the person to get together somewhere private. Let them know that you have been doing deep inner work and that you appreciate who they are in your life and would like to talk to them about something that is very personal to you. Ask them if you can have an hour of their time to talk and to process your thoughts. If it is a friend and they seem nervous, reassure them that you know they aren't a professional but that you value who they are and the safety that you feel with them. It's important that you give them this head's up. And please, don't meet at a Starbucks or a public place. You very well might get emotional, and you don't want your secret overheard by anyone other than your intended confidant.

When I first told my secret of violence, the woman looked at me and said, "Violence is never okay." That did not help me at all. I knew that. And truthfully, I wanted to use my faulty wiring to make her feel bad after she made me feel bad! It was on me though, because I hadn't given her a head's up on the inner work that I'd been doing, and I blurted out my secret while she was driving. It caught her off guard and left me feeling more shameful than I did before I told her. After that, it took me a while to tell someone else.

Have your secret template filled out and with you to refer to or you might go overboard and overshare, especially if you are nervous. However, you do it, keep it to the topic of this one secret so that you don't overwhelm yourself or the other person with your dirty laundry all at once.

When you reveal your secret, it shrinks. The scary monster under the bed is no longer scary. I have heard from countless women that when they finally told, they were met with compassion, love, and even an intimate story about something the other person has experienced. Our true self thrives on being seen and sharing our tender and vulnerable parts. When we show up this way, the faulty wiring no longer leads. Rewiring occurs and we love ourselves and live authentically free.

Gain courage and hope from these women:

I never thought I would tell anyone that I'd been a hi-end prostitute in Vegas. I was hurting and felt like a liar by keeping this from my fiancé. When I told my therapist, she encouraged me to tell him. I did and when we got married, I knew he loved me completely.

***

I couldn't get over the fact that I had slept with my husband's best friend. While I've never revealed it to my husband because it would cause more harm than good, I did tell my friend who also had an affair. We were able to talk about our sadness and regret and share when we had thoughts of temptation. I stopped hating myself and instead of holding back in my relationship with my husband, I began to be his partner.

***

I told my mom that I had stolen her credit card at the height of my addiction and that I was the one who racked up over $10,000 in debt that caused her a lot of turmoil and stress. She was angry at first but appreciated the truth and told me that one time she took $100 from a cash register when she was a waitress. I was floored. We had a good laugh, and I was no longer embarrassed to be around her.

When you think about the secret you are going to share, remember, it's the last time that it will ever be a secret. The grips of shame are shaking in their shoes because they know their time is up. It's time to tell. As I walked this stage of the Secret-Breaking System, I had tremendous relief. The woman who had the angry and violent outburst at the church no longer needed to be defined by that action or believing she needed to be violent to be loved. After I surrendered the secret, I was able to go back to church. And get this, I was even brave enough to go back to the same church where the secret was created and host a table at the Christmas tea! Go true self.

 Our true self thrives on being seen and sharing our tender and vulnerable parts.

The narrative of my false self that told me I wasn't fit to be there, that I was unable to control my rage, and that I was an angry person, simply weren't true. And my true self knew that. She always had. I just couldn't hear her voice because the false self was so loud and so sure of who she thought I was.

For those of you who feel solid with your understanding of Your God, you may only need to put a shiny penny in your pocket to remind yourself that you won't be alone. Your God's got a God-sized solution for your secret. You have your new true self leading the way. You have the collective outpouring of love from hundreds of women who have gone before you.

For those of you who were seeking a power greater than you in Stage Five, Building Your Faith, you can symbolically surrender your secret before you meet with the person. Tie a knot at the top of a bag with your false self and secret in it and take it to the Goodwill drop-off. Your true self is showing up hot and we do not want her derailed by the false self. Ain't nobody got time for that (cue my favorite YouTube video; yes, you can take a two-minute break and watch it).

Part 2: Surrender Your Secret

As you say goodbye to your secret for good, and give it to faith, pick one of the following ways to let it go symbolically.

1. Burn or bury your secret-breaking template.

2. Get a rock or a stone and throw it into a body of water to symbolize washing away the secret.

3. Write a letter to the false self, thanking her for all that she's done for you and for the secret itself. Let her know that your true self will now be leading.

4. Put the secret in Your God box (it can be a shoebox or anything else that might work for you) and shut the lid on it.

5. Talk to Your God about your secret and get a spiritual viewpoint.

A princess with a sad heart took her secret to the mountain. "Mountain," she started, "How do I rid myself of my secret. I cannot bear to look at myself and will bring shame to my people." The princess waited and heard nothing. She rested her forehead on the mountain and said, "Even you mighty mountain, who has protected me from sun, rain, and invaders, are ashamed of me." The mountain shook and the princess was afraid. She turned from the mountain and ran toward the forest. Behind her, rocks crumbled, and rain began to fall. She knew she was being punished for her impurities. She tripped on a log and fell to her knees on the bank of the riverbed. Her reflection in the water was blurred and ugly. She cried as she caught glimpses of her once beautiful face. She raged at the mountain, "Why Mountain, do you forsake me?" In that moment, the earth stopped shaking and the clouds parted. She looked above her and saw the sun. She looked to the river, and it invited her to tell her secret. Trembling and afraid she told the river her story as feelings of unworthiness spilled over her cheeks as tears on her face. When she was empty, the River said, "Now give it to me." The Princess picked up a stone representing the secret and threw it downstream to be carried away. As she walked back to her village, she came to a crossing in the stream where the water had settled. She looked at her image and staring back at her was not an ugly woman, full of shame, but instead, a beautiful, brave, and vibrant warrior princess held her gaze. "This is always who you've been," the river said. And the princess knew it was true. She was a warrior and free of her secret, and she intended to live that way.

Once you tell your trusted person your deep secret, the shame of secret-keeping dissipates and relief replaces worry because your burden is gone. You will no longer have the desire to touch the secret over and over like a pebble in your shoe because it won't define you anymore.

Brave warrior, you are ready to tell!! Let the shame and the shackles fall off your wrists and put your face in the sunlight. You're about to get a new lease on life. As soon as you are done telling, honor your true self and do something that lights you up! You are free now. No more secrets holding you back. Put on that pair of red heels that you've been waiting to wear and go own your life.

Maybe you'd like a glass of wine, or you want to go on a five-mile run. Before you decide, make sure that your true self is in the lead and that your go-to, feel good, isn't being chosen by your false self and its shadow behavior. Take time to contemplate what YOU want to do as this New You. Now that your secret is gone, how will you celebrate? If you have no idea what that might be because everything you're thinking of is somehow doused in the false self, that's really good. Be okay with that. Your true self is getting ready to take ownership and her rightful place in your life. She's about to lead you on an amazing journey, so buckle up. It's going to be a wild ride! Go get it, girl!

Dirty Little Deep Dives

1. Get into action and tell your secret.

2. This is the last time your secret will ever be a secret.

3. You are a warrior.

4. Your true self is taking ownership of your life and that's a good thing.

STAGE EIGHT

Stop Creating Secrets

Girlfriend, I am sending you a high-five followed by a great big hug and a piece of dark chocolate. You did it. You've told one big juicy secret, but we need to wrestle you free of any and all limiting beliefs that kept you lying to yourself and others in the first place. I want you to make working the Secret-Breaking System a habit on all secrets AND even better, get to the place where you are no longer adding any more secrets to your life!

Now that you've told your secret and lived to tell about it, you will start to see the benefits of moving into your true-self life, which was the entire reason you decided to do this work in the first place. Get ready because you are going to stand a little taller, dream a little bigger, and love a little deeper. That fear that you felt over telling your secret is gone. You've told. It's done. It's time to be self-assured and confident as you step into freedom.

To usher in this ascendence to a secret-free you, an understanding of the concepts—limiting beliefs and forgiveness of self—is imperative to move forward. The work in Stage Eight of The Secret Breaking-

System, Stop Creating Secrets, takes a look at all the potential secret-making landmines that might pop up so that you can navigate living in your true self without an implosion. We do this stage to ensure detection of when your false self is trying to lure you back into creating and keeping secrets. As you start learning to live in your true self, you might wonder, *who is this person?* It's you! Your God's love and true nature have always been there but were covered up by your secrets and false self. Now that you're willing to become secret-free, you can discover your gifts, talents, and ways of being that have been camouflaged from view. Instead of secret keeping joy, satisfaction, and bigger living will be the new currency of your life.

You might feel uncomfortable when you start living truthfully. It may feel risky. And you could be tempted to put the cloak of the false self back on. But trust me, the more you practice living in the truth, the less your false self will show up. When she does, although you might be tempted to go backward, you won't to the degree that you once did, because you will intuitively know that your new way of being is so much better.

While our belief system was created during childhood and informs us about the world and how we should behave in relation to it, our limiting beliefs are the overarching umbrella that not only encompass our belief system but also the beliefs that we hold about who we are because of our secrets and from the feedback we have received through experience.

These limiting beliefs are a product of the false self and we need to let them go and forgive ourselves. In part two of the punch, you identified the story you have told yourself about who you are because of the action of the secret. *I'm too mean, a pushover, not worthy, unintelligent, people are out to get me, vulnerable, afraid,* and so on. Limiting beliefs are also the guardrails we put up that keep us in place. *I'm too fat, too skinny, too nice, too bold, too much,* fill in the blank. At their core, limiting beliefs are any beliefs that you hold about yourself or the world that keep you stuck. They can extend to beliefs about groups of people, society, and individuality. Limiting beliefs are particularly important to look out for because they keep you stuck in place, believing that you can't do more than you are already doing.

The false self is powerful and will not only rope in the critical narrator but will also bring in your childhood belief system and any unkindness's that you believe about yourself, to keep you from fully becoming your true self.

Here are some overarching examples of limiting beliefs:

- People like me can't do that.

- I don't come from a scholastic family.

- I weigh too much.

- I am unlovable.

- I am unworthy.

- The world isn't a safe place.

- People are out to get me.

- Nothing good ever happens for me.

- Something is inherently wrong with me.

- I have to have a degree to do that

- I have the wrong degree to do that.

- I married the wrong man to ever be truly happy.

- I don't work hard so I won't ever have money.

Limiting beliefs create a ceiling that we live under, and they suffocate us and leave little room for exploration. You have told one secret and your true self is seeing that the limiting beliefs she once held aren't true. Your false self is still right behind her and is trying to lead you to think demeaning thoughts like, *what's wrong with me? I'm not good enough. I can't do that. I won't find love.* These thoughts can drive us back to secret actions and secret-keeping. Keep working the Secret-Breaking System on all your past secrets while setting up your life for creating no more secrets.

As women, we've all heard about the proverbial glass ceiling. You know how it was created? By our limiting beliefs. We need to put on our red heels and shatter the ceiling because those beliefs aren't true and are no longer useful. Limiting beliefs come in all shapes and sizes. They are the ideas and messages that keep us living in our circumstances. When we change our perception of who we could be by even 5 percent, our world changes. We see what we desire differently, which causes us to react and participate in life in a confident way. In our false self, we would think a thought, decide it was true based on a limiting belief, and then take an action on it that created a secret. In hope of us getting to a root feeling. In our true self, we challenge the belief without latching into our faulty feelings and take an action that will keep us free from secrets.

For much of my life I subconsciously believed that I would get a divorce before my seventh year of marriage. My parents divorced after that amount of time, and I assumed I would too. This belief was also a secret because can you imagine me telling my husband, look I'll marry you but it's probably only going to last seven years? This belief condoned my unkind behavior toward my husband those first seven years because we were going to get a divorce anyway. When anniversary seven came and went, I was able to let that limiting belief go.

Your limiting beliefs don't have to take seven more years to change. You can start challenging those beliefs now and taking new actions today.

Here are some limiting beliefs that women have shared with me and their course correction to true self:

Jenny spent her entire life watching her mom take the backseat to the kids. Naturally, Jenny emulated this same behavior when she was a mom. She put her dream of starting her own business on hold in lieu of staying home to raise the kids so that she could do it right. She made light of wanting her own business and kept the secret that deep down she wanted more ownership of her life. One day, her friend who was also a mom, told her she was launching a business. When Jenny asked her what about her kids, her friend confidently said that they would be happier if she was happier. Jenny saw her limiting belief based on her mom's life, and her friend gave her the courage to start her own business.

***

Elora had an unconscious belief that she wasn't good enough to ever be in the leadership role at an organization. She was often praised along her career path for how well she did in support roles and how thankful people were to have her in those roles. About ten years into her career there was a job opening that she wanted. It was for a management position which was something she had never done before. She wanted to go for it but secretly believed that she wouldn't be able to do the job. When she found out that a colleague who was in a position lower than her was going to apply, it blew her mind. How could she jump the ranks like that? When she asked her in a snarky way what she was thinking, the colleague told her that if she didn't take control over her own happiness how would she get it? That forever changed her limited thinking about her own role of leadership, and the assertive employment actions she took after that.

***

Natalie believed that people who asked for help were weak and stupid. One day her son was asking for help with fitting the trash bag on the container. She told him to figure it out. He was frustrated and having trouble. Her husband went to him and kindly explained and showed him how to do it. She felt terrible about the way she'd treated him. One day she was struggling with something, and her husband asked if she needed help. Her immediate response was to say no but she said yes instead. It was in that moment that she no longer thought of herself or others as stupid or weak for needing help. She shattered a limiting belief that had blocked intimacy and community.

When you challenge your limiting beliefs, your world can change, and it can aid you in breaking free from your old secret-keeping behavior. When my seven-year anniversary came and went and we were still married, I changed as a wife. I was softer, more loving, more present, and I stopped being such a jerk because I had been wrong about my limiting belief that we would divorce. I was able to truly challenge the belief of my thinking and replace it with a God-centered partnership, which allowed my true self to lead. And boy, did she know how to be married in a much saner and loving way than my false self. Letting go of limiting beliefs makes room for a new way of living that doesn't involve keeping secrets.

This courageous woman challenged her limiting beliefs and found love:

> *Jessica used to believe that single women over forty would never find a good partner and would only end up raising someone else's kids. When she challenged the belief, she knew that it wasn't 100 percent true. Her friend Amanda was forty-one and just got married to a man that she was crazy about who loved and respected her and who didn't have kids. When she thought about Amanda, she decided that if she could find love, so could Jessica. Jessica decided to take a small step and went out with a few different men that she was set up with. The first two were duds, but she went anyway. With the new belief that it wasn't 100 percent true that she wouldn't find anyone she also posted a dating profile. She was scared but she remembered when she was lonely in college and joined a skiing club to make friends and was still in contact with some of them twenty years later. She took that past experience where she had a similar feeling and applied it to her limiting belief. Eighteen months later, Jessica was engaged and no longer living under the pretense of her false self.*

When we are willing to define or challenge our limiting beliefs, magic happens. Let's find yours.

Part 1: Defining Your Limiting Beliefs

1. Identify and write down a limiting belief that you have about yourself that holds you back.

2. Challenge the belief by asking yourself if it's 100 percent true. If you can't think of an instance in your own life where it isn't true, think about other people you know or have heard about and look for places where it might not be true. Write down your findings.

3. If it's not 100 percent true, what could you believe instead? What else?

4. If you believed that, what action would you take?

5. If you took that action, what might happen?

6. If it feels hard, unlikely, or uncomfortable to take this step, think about another time in your life when you did something that you didn't think you could do. What did you learn from that experience that you can apply to this?

While our belief system was created during childhood and informs us about the world and how we should behave in relation to it, our limiting beliefs are the overarching umbrella that not only encompass our belief system but also the beliefs that we hold about who we are because of our secrets and from the feedback we have received through experience.

Forgiveness of self is the cornerstone to letting go of the false self. When we forgive ourselves for the limiting beliefs that turned into a critical narrative, that then turned into secret actions, that ultimately created big secrets, we let go of the identity of the false self. Take a deep exhale while you pause and let the weight of that sink in. Forgiveness is the antithesis of the false self and breaks the secret-keeping and making cycle. When we truly and completely forgive ourselves, we stop the mind trash in our heads and focus on more productive lives—ones filled with love and prosperous actions.

When you don't forgive yourself, it means that the limiting beliefs of the false self still have a grip on you. The limiting beliefs and lies that the false self tells you still seem true and if that's what's happening you will continue to live a false life built on secrets. You may have told one secret, or maybe even a few, but if you still have areas where you think you are a piece of crap, less than, or that you don't deserve true happiness and freedom, you will be trapped by new crappy actions that develop a new batch of secrets. We do enough laundry! We don't need to keep putting secrets through the wash! Forgiving yourself might seem impossible but courageous warrior, you got this. It's time to lean in. You can throw away the old script and write a new one. In Sharpie. Your true self knows more and is a reliable source who can guide you onto higher ground. She can't do it if you don't forgive because the power of the limiting beliefs will not allow her to come forward.

I cannot stress the importance of forgiving yourself enough. If you don't, you will be tempted to beat yourself up and may even believe you don't deserve forgiveness. When I blurted out my secret and was told that violence was never okay, I shrunk back. My false self grew a little bigger and her limiting beliefs seemed safer than a new way of being. It took time for me to forgive myself completely for the violence. My false self was firmly grounded in her identity. I felt shame and undeserving of forgiveness. What I had done felt too big to let go of.

I was out with my dad for lunch one day and I admiringly told him what a badass he had always been. He looked at me with a reserved sadness.

"No, Gretchen. I was never a badass. That's not who I am."

I was floored and even argued with him a little about it.

"Yes, you are dad. You were always the guy who won the fight."

"I didn't even like to fight," he said.

I was shocked. Here was my badass dad telling me that his past behavior wasn't who he really was. If he wasn't a tough guy, what did that mean about my false self's faulty wiring that violence equaled love? What did it mean about my limiting belief that I thought I was a badass in my own way? My dad put his hand over mine.

"I'm a lover, and so are you. We have to forgive ourselves." That was my turning point. I got in the car and cried. My dad saw me as I really was. I could see her too. I was loving. I was kind. I didn't like violence. I wasn't scary. As I forgave myself for the secret of the almost stabbing, my limiting beliefs lifted. I was amazed at how untrue they had always been. I could think of many circumstances where my true self had shown up, where I was kind, extended love, was funny and playful, and liked to be with people. I wish I could say it was an overnight process where I shed the shame of how long I held this belief, but it took a while. Awareness kept me from making more secrets with violent or angry behavior.

 Forgiveness is the antithesis of the false self and breaks the secret-keeping and making cycle

You might be wondering how in the world you can forgive yourself for what you've done. You may still think that your secret is too awful to forgive. The good news is that without you realizing it, the forgiveness process started back in Stage One when you took the first step and opened this book. Each stage in the Secret-Breaking System was designed to help you forgive yourself a little bit at a time. As your false self has become exposed with its hard outer shell and soft underbelly, your true self who is strong, vibrant, and courageous, has begun to emerge. Each secret-breaking stage required brave actions. Each action has supported your true self. That kind of support is synonymous with self-forgiveness. As you let go of the final bits of your false self, let's thank her for all of the ways that she has served you and forgive her for where she led you off course. She has worked hard to protect you, but she can rest now. Your true self is ready.

Part 2: Forgiveness of the False Self

1. Write a letter to your false self thanking her for all that she's done to protect you, the secrets she held close to keep you safe, and the actions she's taken to help you thrive. Let her know that your true self can take care of her now and that her faulty wiring, limiting beliefs and secret-keeping are no longer needed. Grant her forgiveness for what she did and didn't know. Assure her that you are committed to stepping into a secret-free life full of purpose.

2. Visualize your false self walking on the beach, playing in the sand, carefree, alive, and happy.

When we don't forgive ourselves, we leave a door open for our false self to come through. It's time to close that door. While you've been working on cultivating new qualities, your false self has been doing pushups in the other room so that she can be ready to spring into action at a moment's notice. Your true self doesn't need her protection anymore. You've told the truth about one secret but if you don't forgive yourself your limiting beliefs you will be back on the secret train. When you forgive yourself, your ability to connect with others, yourself, and Your God will increase.

 Forgiveness of self is the cornerstone to letting go of the false self.

But what if you are upset with God? What if you feel like you were forgotten, betrayed, or unseen because of the terrible events that happened to you that caused you to keep secrets. Or what if you are willing to forgive yourself but you don't think Your God will forgive you because your secret is so big? To shine your inner spiritual light, you may either need to ask Your God for forgiveness or decide to forgive Your God. A simple prayer can work for either situation. You can ask Your God daily for the courage to step into your true self through the Secret-Breaking System. You can use the below prayer or write one of your own to help you with forgiveness.

> *God help me to not just remove my secrets to be a better me but help me forgive all who were in those secrets, including myself. Show me that You are here to love me completely regardless of how I show up on any given day. (If needed you can add, please help me with my faith, forgiveness, and trust in you).*

On the flip side of forgiveness of self is unforgiveness for others who have been part of our secret-keeping life. When we have an unforgiving heart, we carry the person we're upset with like a heavy twenty-pound sack of potatoes around our waist, everywhere we go. We can't shape a new future while we are carrying the past. By not forgiving we limit ourselves. We are holding on to the hurts and they keep us chained. And here's the deal, everyone is at fault and no one is to blame. Including you. Those people who hurt you, they were reading from their own script, living in their false self, keeping their own secrets. How about this for a compassion check? They had their own one-two-three punch and critical narrator running the show on their quest for their own root feelings.

What if I don't want to forgive? It's a fair question. But it is being asked by your false, lower self. Remember that. When someone hurts us and we stay upset about it, we feel like we have earned the right to that feeling. And we have. But you don't need it anymore. The negative feeling is taking up space where a more empowering feeling could reside. People hurt us, they betray us, and the unspeakable acts that have harmed us aided in making us secret-keepers. It's true. I'm validating all your experiences, but it's time to let them go. Stage Eight won't be full circle complete until you stop holding grudges.

The slippery slope of the justification we feel from our resentment keeps us in false self-living. We think that our grudge and unforgiveness are payback to the person who has messed up our lives, but truthfully, it hurts us more. The payback is like a boomerang that keeps hitting us in the face and then drops at our feet. We energetically send it back out but the negativity, pain, hurt, rage, and remorse that it takes with it always comes back to us and gains steam every time we touch it with our thoughts, reliving, and storytelling about who we are because of it.

Forgiveness of others is powerful. It gives you a platform to step out of victimhood and into ownership and realize that you have lived long enough with the consequences. You decide you are ready to let go of the past and its wheel of hurts and disappointments and get busy creating your kick-ass life. But you can't have it both ways. You can't live with unforgiveness and choose freedom. The resentments will always pull you back into the limiting beliefs of the false self.

A special note on what forgiveness is not. Forgiveness is in no way condoning what the other person did. I would never want you to deny or gloss over the facts of the situation and how it affected your life, that just perpetuates more secret-keeping. Instead, forgiveness will help you move forward and live without constraint. When we have unforgiving hearts, the person who hurt us still holds power over our lives because we are holding a resentment against them for what they did that caused us to keep secrets. If we're carrying unforgiveness, we carry our secrets. And we've carried our secrets long enough.

Forgiving others takes empathy, courage, and the willingness to let the last remnants of your secret go. To forgive another person is an internal release and, it's a process. Making a decision to forgive someone is a start. Maybe you are able to forgive one part of what someone did to you in the secret you told but not another aspect of the offense. Or maybe it's easier to forgive one person in your life who betrayed or hurt you but harder to forgive another person who did something similar. Don't judge yourself for the resistance or ease you experience during the forgiveness process. As you begin to forgive, your heart will change, and it will become easier to live a life where you do not become easily offended or hurt.

As you start to forgive on just this one secret, I encourage you to try to have an empathetic viewpoint about the person who hurt you. It will help you to be able to shift from the hardness in your heart to a place of neutrality and sometimes even compassion. If you are unable to access these feelings, it's okay. You can start with the willingness to want to forgive and allow compassion to show up. It can take days, months, and even years to shift to this perspective but it does not need to stop you from forgiving the person who is a part of your secret.

 You can't live with unforgiveness and choose freedom. The resentments will always pull you back into the limiting beliefs of the false self.

Sexual abuse survivors or anyone who has suffered physical, emotional, or other forms of abuse may struggle deeply with forgiving the person who did these unspeakable acts, as well as the possible others who knew and were complicit. I completely empathize that forgiveness when we have been violated, especially as a child, seems like a herculean task. Take your time and forgive in baby steps in your heart. Remember that the forgiveness of others is for you and your true self, not for the benefit of the perpetrator. I encourage you to seek professional help from a therapist or trusted counsel should you need it.

Forgiveness can be given face to face or can be done simply in your heart without any contact. Here are some stories from women who decided to forgive. Let their experience give you hope.

I wasn't going to forgive my ex-best friend for talking behind my back and telling my boyfriend that I had been unfaithful in my last relationship. He broke up with me because of it and I hated her for it. The truth is that while what she did was wrong, it had been ten years since we spoke, and I was married with two kids. The ex-didn't matter and the story

I kept telling myself that I wasn't good enough to keep a boyfriend or a best friend was only hurting me. I decided that I was done holding on to the anger and the story and forgave her. I envisioned her happy, healthy, and in a loving relationship. I looked at photos of us from college and truly wished her well from afar. It made room in my heart for another friendship.

***

I was never going to forgive my ex for giving me herpes. We had been together for three years when I had an outbreak and found out he was cheating on me. I broke up with him but the secrets that were created were that I was now rotten goods, no one would ever want to be in a relationship with me, and that I was so boring that even if they were, they would cheat on me. I stayed in this story for years. One day a guy I was dating who I really cared about told me that he wanted to get to know me deeper but that I made it impossible because my heart was hard. That hit me like a ton of bricks. And he was right. My heart was hard. I looked at my ex-boyfriend's Facebook account. He was married and had kids. He wasn't thinking about what he'd done to me. He went on to live a happy life. This enraged me. I was still living with the pain and the shame of his actions. When I told a friend about my secret of having herpes and feeling like no one would ever love me because I was boring, she encouraged me to forgive my ex and myself for what had happened when we were so young. I found a photo of my ex and I from when we were twenty years old and almost didn't recognize myself. I was happy and lighthearted. My eyes were bright. I wanted that version of me back, albeit a little smarter and wiser. I wrote a letter to him telling him that I forgave him and to myself asking for forgiveness for how I had treated us for so long and giving forgiveness to the young woman who didn't know any better. I burned both letters and called the guy I had been dating and told him that the reason I had been holding back was that I had herpes. I put it on the table. We are still dating.

**

After being molested by my uncle I thought I would never be whole. I was so angry at all men and especially at God. How could God let that happen to me? What had I done that was so wrong that He would let a young girl be victimized by such a sicko? Being molested affected my entire life. I had an identity crisis, didn't trust men, thought that I was bisexual only to find out that I wasn't. I kept secrets on top of secrets about who I was, what I wasn't and told myself that I would always be alone. One day I was at a group for survivors of molestation, and I heard a woman talk about forgiving herself, her perpetrator, and God. I thought this was a wild and ridiculous idea, but I was intrigued. She went on to say that she did it in steps. First, she forgave herself, then she forgave the perpetrator, and lastly, she forgave God. She said she imagined the perpetrator as his childlike self and knew that his intent was not to harm her. She imagined herself as a child and knew that she could not have made a choice that would have protected her. Finally, she said that God had never abandoned her or turned His head or covered His eyes. He was open and available to her at any time and was so sad *that something so terrible had happened to her. Hearing that, I lost it. I cried and cried and let the tears go. I went home and prayed to God to help me with my unforgiving heart. The story about who I was shifted after that. I realized I had never allowed myself to cry or express it. I had walked around under the title of "victim" and while I was, it was one small piece of the rest of my great big story, and I was ready to step into that. I got therapy and together we created a way for me to forgive God by getting to know Him in a new way.*

Keep breathing girlfriend, the heavy stuff is almost done. You've decided to let go of your limiting beliefs. You've forgiven yourself. You are forgiving others and your true self is taking the lead. To help make the transition easier, let's take a look at the other potential secret-keeping traps. Here's a list of landmines to watch out for that left unnoticed can cause secret-keeping. When you know what to look out for you are less likely to pick up your old ways of being and more likely to stay in your true self.

Secret Keeping Landmines

Habits

Our secret-keeping habits like procrastination, intimidation, lack of follow-through, and other perceived ways of being crop up and we have to cover our tracks. The easiest and quickest way to do that is to tell a lie to not get found out. Thus, creating a secret. Good or bad, we use habits, as an excuse to act in the ways of the false self and they get us in and out of jams. Catch yourself anytime you think, well that's just the way I am. That is the lie of the false self. You are not your habit, and your true self knows it.

Expectations and Disappointments

Expectations are premeditated resentments. It's like drinking poison and wanting someone else to die. When you have an expectation, you aren't in an agreement with the other person. You are just expecting them to do whatever it is you are wanting them to do and then getting upset when it doesn't happen. You take that upset and build a story about what it means for you, for them, and for the relationship when nothing was ever truly communicated. Hence you harbor secret feelings about this person and therefore become consumed with your resentment which blocks you from being your true realized self. When people don't come through, we double down and become resistant to trusting others. Instead of letting go and letting the consequences be whatever they are going to be, we become controlling, passive-aggressive, and manipulative to get our way because we've decided on the importance of our expectations. We have held on so tight to other people, places, and things that they have figurative scratch marks down their backs. Having expectations leads to disappointment that can cause us to engage in actions that lead to secret-keeping. Letting go of expectations is pivotal for breaking your habit of keeping secrets.

Fear

Our fears, most of the time, are like nightmares in the closet. We make up stories and worst-case scenarios based on situations that will probably never come to be. We have weird thoughts based on fear that lead us astray and back to secret-keeping. We fear who we think we should be and can't measure up to. We care about what others think of us. We need others to validate that we matter and to fill in our insecurities and the holes in our souls. It doesn't work. People are having their own human experience and are going to fail us. Looking for others to make us okay is always a losing situation because of our fear our thinking becomes clouded. We are afraid of our circumstances and take actions based on fear instead of faith to fix our problems. When we can face our fears by telling another or our God and creating a logical plan, our minds can release our made-up scenarios. We can divert fear to let go of secret-keeping tendencies.

Worry

We are so worried about the other shoe dropping that we cut off our own happiness instead of living and playing life full out. We worry about aging, our kids getting older, losing a job, our bodies changing, turning into our mothers, death, parenthood, retirement, being single, getting married, and the list goes on and on. We internalize these feelings as secrets. Living in worry and anxiety creates secret-keeping. Worry would have us pick up our old script of the false self with its old tools and limiting beliefs ways to protect us. We fear that if we stop worrying, we will miss something that we should have seen or prevented. The truth is what we worry about aren't usually never happens. It's something else that gets exposed. The subtlety we weren't expecting. We give up years of our lives thinking, plotting, imagining, and living in scenarios and situations that have never happened. Worry robs us of peace, joy, being present, opportunities, and purpose. Worry itself, often becomes a secret.

EGO

Edging God out. Anytime you find yourself thinking that you can do it on your own, you don't need anyone, especially Your God, you are in EGO. Ego can make us spew the silliest lies and keep the best secrets because Ego has us believe that we're in charge and have power. Sometimes, Ego is right; we are creating our circumstances with every thought and action we take. Ego limits our God connection and tells us that we don't need anyone outside of self. And that's a lie. Our best thinking created secret-keepers.

Unreliable Narrators

Your false self tells you stories based on emotional disturbances. Giving too much authority to our emotions based on our internal narrative will create secrets. We tell ourselves stories all day long that are full of misinformation, emotion, and nonlogical thinking. We then base our lives on these stories that are told to us by an unreliable narrator who speaks to us based on emotion. If we're winning, we're great. If we're losing, we're terrible. People make huge choices based on fickle emotion rather than stable footing. When the unreliable narrator makes decisions, we are sure to keep and create secrets.

With so many ways to create secrets, it's important to stay honest about your behavior so that you don't backslide into your false self. To stay clean—have integrity—with your true self, it can be helpful to create a daily routine where you look at your thoughts, actions and behaviors. By doing this, you will catch a secret before it takes root and causes serious consequences. It's normal and so easy to tell a little lie and think a nasty thought. Being honest with yourself will help you to see how far you've come and will serve as a warning sign if you have gotten off course.

Part 3: Daily Secret–Creating Check In

1. Did I keep or create any secrets today?

2. If so, what root or tripwire feeling, faulty wiring, or limiting belief was at play?

When I say do this daily, I mean daily! Staying clean with secret-keeping is akin to breaking a long-standing love affair. It will take time, repetition, dedication, and honesty. By no means are you expected to drop all of your false self behaviors and ways of thinking overnight. As you practice letting your true self lead, you will notice that you like who you are and how you feel and what you think. You will begin to trust your true self and one day, she will be leading without any effort or thought, and you will be so glad to be hitched to her little red wagon because you will love the direction that she's taking you. In the spirit of letting her lead, we are going to learn more about your true self so that you can be comfortable giving her the driver's seat. In Stage Nine of the Secret Breaking System: Death of the Old You, you are going to learn who your true self is and you will fall in love and be giddy with excitement about all things that make up you, wonderful and special, you!

Dirty Little Deep Dives

1. It's time for you to put on your red heels and shatter the limiting beliefs of your glass ceiling.

2. Be gentle with your false self and thank her, truly, deeply, and completely for all that she's done for you so that you can make room for your true self.

3. Forgiveness is the cornerstone to letting go of the false self.

4. Watch out for secret-keeping landmines by doing a dally secret-creating check-in.

STAGE NINE

Death of the Old You

We come in from the streets of secret-keeping from castles and gutters that are full of gossip, adrenaline, half-truths, storytelling, and electricity. We've built lives, fires, and careers off the back of our false self and her secrets. It's been anything but boring. Our secrets have been a part of our make-up, like cigarette smoke that you can't get out of your hair or your clothes after a night out. Secrets cling to the false self who doesn't want to give up her place in your world. Her intentions hint of nobility—to protect you—but she tirelessly tries to hold you back from any chance of change.

Here's the good news, by Stage Nine, you already have changed. You've seen it for yourself by the softening that's occurred from you uncovering secrets. You've noticed a difference in your confidence level, and you now have a seed of hope that you can, in fact, reach higher. To get there, we need to drill down further and identify your lingering triggers so that they don't have the chance to ambush you and take you off track. It will also be important to identify the values of the New You so that you can see them clearly and use them as guideposts to inform the way you make decisions and to keep you on the road to a secret-free life.

To thrive in your new skin, you have to quit your false self once and for all, and Stage Nine contains the final steps to do just that. To kick your false self out like a bad roommate or that one-night stand that stayed too long, you can no longer open the door to let her in anymore. Not even a crack! If you do, she will slink by you and wiggle her way back into the lead.

No more hedging.

No more backup plans.

No looking back.

She's out.

I know the two of you have had some fun together. If we're honest, you're like besties gone bad. You have to let her go and get a restraining order if you need to. Your false self is disastrous and only causes confusion, chaos, and the creation of more secrets. At this point in the Secret-Breaking System, you are looking for higher waters, but you can't get there if she's still holding onto your legs. You will drown.

In Stage Nine, Death of the Old You, we're going to have a party! A birthday party to celebrate the birth-day of the New You! This is the day you say goodbye to your old ways of being and step into the New You with your head held high and with love in your heart. Your key action here is to completely let go of your false self within the Old You while simultaneously ushering in and getting to know the New You. Rest assured; you have already done more of the letting go than you might realize.

Being the New You is exhilarating. Finally, you can step into a bigger container where you can explore the depths of all of your glorious intricacies and wonderful oddities that make you, you! Here's the breakdown: your Old You was made of one-part true self and one-part false self. They were constantly at odds with one another and battling over who should lead your life. Your New You is 100 percent, authentically you, owns her power, knows what she likes and doesn't like, and is interested in self-discovery. The Old You was driven by the false self's fear from old patterns and habits and had little time to find her true identity. Your New You is ready to say goodbye to this outdated version of who you once were. Your New You is prepared to move forward with no regrets. If you're feeling excited, this *is* exciting. If you're feeling some sadness or anxiety over letting go of the Old You, that's okay. Be kind, but don't stare at the past or give her too much sympathy. She's had her heyday. Now it's time for the New You to live in the sun.

One of the gifts of letting go of the Old You is that you will have more time to truly live. And as women, we know that time is a hot commodity! You will no longer be losing hours of your life in manipulative, coercive, sneaky behaviors that created secrets and lies. There will no longer be a need to cover up your actions. Your life will be more vibrant, steady, and even. Want to know the best part? You will have the ability to create your great big life rather than maintaining and protecting your secrets.

Ummmm . . . is that it?

Maybe you're looking for a sexier payoff.

You might be thinking that the New You sounds kind of boring and too stable. You may even convince yourself that you like your life of secrets and their sense of danger or mystery. Girlfriend, you've been duped because that life was a life of disaster and misery! Surviving on scraps. Don't believe me, go back and read the journal you kept with your answers to the exercises. That should be all the evidence you need to remind yourself that what I'm saying is true. You deserve more. In fact, you were made for it.

What the New You is offering is a sustainable life that you will love, even on the crappy days. You won't want to trade it for the exhaustive mind-spinning behavior of your old false self. And I get it, the Old You is hard to let go of especially for those of you with a more addictive personality. Secrets can be like a drug, and you, their slave. As much as we want to let go of them, the addiction to drama can be hard to walk away from, making letting go of the Old You, difficult.

That's why we are going to rehab. Together.

When I stopped being a secret-keeper, being tough still tempted me. Come to find out, some of the false self was lingering in my New You because I hadn't committed to letting her go 100 percent. The nagging question, who am I going to be if I'm not tough, gnawed at my mind. At first when I shed my old shell, I was embarrassed to be soft and kind and to not use sarcasm as a way of navigating the world. I felt weak. And I didn't understand how I would get my needs met if people weren't intimidated by me anymore. I felt dull. Life was boring and flat. No big ups or downs. No drama. No adrenaline.

 Your New You is 100 percent, authentically you, owns her power, knows what she likes and doesn't like, and is interested in self-discovery.

The electricity in my life was gone because I was no longer riding the current of violence equaling love. I stopped disguising humor with insults. I was a person of my word and could no longer lie (because that would create new secrets) to get out of plans that I didn't want to keep. I had to walk a straight line, but it felt more like wearing a straitjacket. At that point, I wasn't convinced that a life without secrets was worth it. I was shaky on my feet, and it was hard to live in this new way without picking up my old tools for survival and if I'm honest, I missed them. I was really good at using them and I hadn't figured out what to replace them with yet that didn't feel completely boring.

No gossip? No meanness? No bullying? No flirting?

Sigh, what was I supposed to do?

Take up knitting?

Was this new life worth it? Really? Come to find out, it was. I had to sit in the uncomfortableness of not knowing how to behave or which tools to use until my New You took charge. And when she did, it was mind-blowing. I found a new person in me that had gifts and talents buried and unreaped. Who knew? She did. And guess what, the more my New You led, the better my relationships became.

Just this year, I was in the car with my two teenaged sons and their girlfriends, and I said something about being tough.

"Mom, you aren't tough. You're soft," my younger son said.

I had an inner moment where I wanted to contest his claim. Was I slacking? Should I start to crack the whip again in the house? Was I a pushover? My Old You was knocking at the door, dying to come back in. I remained vigilant and accepted what my son saw with happiness. It's been years since I've been a secret keeper and my old identity can still trick me into thinking that it's who I am today even when it's not. I spent a lot of time on self-discovery, figuring out who I am, what I like, what I was obligated to, and my values. The more I learned about myself, the clearer my life became. I still got tangled up from time to time in old ways of thinking and would catch myself and have to reset. It can be especially difficult to let go of the Old You with the people you are closest with, but if you stick to it, you can and will do it. Stage Nine is by no means trying to turn you into the perfect human, but if you'd like to be Mother Theresa, by all means. Instead, this stage allows you access to the full picture of who you are, aging lines and all.

Acceptance of self is powerful. It eliminates the falsities we've lived with that have defined us for so long and replaces them with authenticity and truth. Knowing who you are on a cellular level will change everything.

In the beginning stages of finding the New You, you will primarily use the tool of contrary action. What is contrary action? It's taking an action that you wouldn't normally take so that you can create a new action that will lead to a new internal narrative. The way it works is that you will no longer take action based on your faulty wiring. Instead, you will lean on your New You to lead you to take contrary action even if it feels awkward.

If you usually speak up or argue, it could mean that you practice the pause and take a beat before responding. If you are usually quiet, it could mean speaking up. If you are inclined to over commit or overdo to find self-worth, practice waiting to commit for twenty-four hours. If you are prone to depressive feelings that leave you on the couch eating cheese-flavored popcorn, take a shower, go for a walk, or call a friend. Grab your journal or punch a punching bag. If you have lost your connection with God, pray. The options are plentiful and will not lead to shadow behaviors that create more secrets. In the beginning your Old You will argue that she is sure that your contrary action isn't the right answer and will try to activate your faulty wiring to get you into motion. You can notice her messages and allow them to float by without getting hooked in. Then allow yourself to try a new tool and see how it works. You may not use it perfectly, but as you begin to take new actions, you will change and the New You will gain her footing as your Old You loses power.

What you must do first though is make a firm commitment that no matter what, you are not going to allow the Old You to lead. This is a life-or-death situation, and it needs to be taken seriously. If you let her crack the door, she will ultimately kick it in and push your New You out the window. She will woo you, call you back, comfort you, and mesmerize you with all the reasons as to why the New You is doing it wrong. It's imperative that you firmly decide that this is it, the Old You is gone. No matter what, you are never to behave in those old ways of being again. They are no longer acceptable, nor do they serve.

The day came when I had to choose between the Old You and New You in real time. The door had cracked open. My husband had not kept his word about going with me to an event and my Old You was ready to lose it on him. Humiliating and unkind words were on the tip of my tongue. My hands were looking for papers that I could scatter off of his desk. My insides were shaking with adrenaline and my tripwire of abandonment was activated. My false self was chasing her root feelings again. As I stood there, I had a moment of clarity. I could do what I had always done and use the ways of the Old You and create more shameful secrets, or I could choose to do something new and step into my New You. I took a breath to regulate my internal system, took contrary action, and said, "Okay. If you change your mind, you can meet me there."

There were so many contrary actions in this:

- I took a breath to activate the pause button.

- This allowed me to regulate myself.

- I kept my hands and my words to myself.

- I left the house in my New You with dignity and grace.

I picked up the keys and left. I sobbed in the car because my rage had nowhere to go. I went to the stupid party without him and bad-mouthed him to others, but I hadn't been violent toward him with my words or physically. My New You knew something that I didn't. I had made progress. Even though I was scared of the outcome because my tripwire of being abandoned had been activated and my faulty wiring of violence equals love wanted to rise up, I had firmly decided I would not behave in the ways of my Old You. Regardless of what my husband would or wouldn't do, my new behavior was ultimately about me, and I could learn how to have my root feeling of wanting love met by loving myself. I could love myself by not creating secrets and shameful behavior. Guess what happened? He showed up two hours later to the party and we had a good time. There have been many times since in our marriage that I have gone places without him, without making it a big deal, or turning it into a fight, or fantasizing about divorce. Sometimes he meets me there and sometimes he doesn't. Either way, I am okay. My New You is not easily abandoned. She knows that her root feeling of wanting love is fulfilled because she gives that to herself.

Powerful.

That was a turning point for me and there will be a turning point for you. Be ready and use my story to anchor yourself. We were all put here for a unique reason. We can't access the reason if we are fumbling around in our Old You ways. You have Purpose. Power. Potential. It's time to live up to it and set your world ablaze with your beauty, uniqueness, and glory. *How* becomes the question? When you no longer have your old secret-keeping ways to navigate through life with, what do you use instead? You may be surprised, in the very best way, at all that is available to you.

Part 1: Know Your Triggers

It's important for you to know what trips you up so that when your Old You is activated, you can take contrary action. Think of your secret and use the work you have already done in Stages One to Eight to crystalize the following:

1. What is your faulty wiring (reference Stage Two, Part One)?

2. What is your tripwire emotion (reference Stage Two, Part Two)?

3. What is your root feeling (reference Stage Three, Part One)?

4. What is another way to get your root feeling met? Hint, it is never by acting in your Old Self.

To let go of the Old You in her entirety, you have to be prepared when she shows up. If you are triggered, that's your cue to double down and to take a new action by letting go of your false self.

Letting go of the Old You requires getting to know the New You at the highest level. The superficial basics of who you are that are on display are only a small portion of the whole picture. No matter where you are in the process of knowing the New You, the real you, who has always been there, we are going to roll up our sleeves and uncover your inner workings so that you can live on stable ground.

Even on your worst day, I want you to say this mantra to yourself:

I am Purposeful. I am Powerful. I have unlimited Potential.

If I can reiterate anything enough times, no matter what stage you are on in the system, don't create more secrets. Even if you feel yourself slipping back, it's okay. Work the stage in the system that you are struggling with and then repeat this mantra. This is your chance to step in and to get to know you. Take the development of the New You seriously. You will see a new way of living start to take shape.

You have Purpose. Power. Potential. It's time to live up to it and set your world ablaze with your beauty, uniqueness, and glory.

As you experience what might feel like a loss of identity, you will begin to define yourself in new and more empowering ways that will create a purpose-filled current that isn't based on the opinions of others or the old stories you've been telling yourself about who you are. For many of us, we've put the needs of others before ours for so long that we are disconnected from our own thoughts and feelings. We've gone numb to our inner truths, and we check out and distract ourselves from our purpose with electronics, shopping, eating, spending, drinking, and being busy. We've buried parts of ourselves behind our secrets and we've told ourselves stories that have kept us in place.

These women embraced their New You voice:

> *As Anna began to get to know who she was, she was shocked at how hard it was to answer questions about what she truly wanted and cared about in an honest way. Her old ways of being that told her she was rude and loud and that no one would ever trust her kept showing up. She had to let the voices have their turn without getting her feelings involved. Once her feelings were engaged, she knew she was a goner and would start making decisions that lead to secret-keeping instead of purpose.*

*** *

Peggy had a big truth she needed to share that she was positive would end up in divorce. She could not stand her in-laws and had no desire to invest time into creating a relationship with them. When she admitted this truth to herself, she felt like a horrible person. She also knew that she could no longer go on seeing them each and every week. As a people pleaser who was afraid of rocking the boat, she was scared to tell her husband. There was a moment that she knew it did not matter what his reaction would be because she could not keep seeing them as often as she was. She told him expecting the worst, and even though he was upset, he understood. They compromised and Peggy vested them twice a month instead of weekly. She took painting classes on the other weeks. For her it was luxurious.

Part 2: Getting to Know You

It's time to get real and to explore the hidden crevices of who you are. Answer the following questions as honestly as possible. They range in depth and are meant to help you to become curious about who you are. Allow yourself to go with your gut when you answer. Give yourself time to thoroughly answer the questions. Self-discovery is a gift and shouldn't be rushed.

1. What comes naturally to you?

2. What do people come to you for?

3. What's your superpower (something that you do better than most people)?

4. What do you like the most about yourself?

5. What causes/organizations do you care about?

6. Where do you feel called to give back?

7. What talents do you have?

8. What are your gifts?

9. What people, places, and situations do you feel the most energized from?

10. What hidden dream or desire do you keep coming back to even if you haven't taken action on it?

11. What inklings do you have about what you are here to do?

Getting to know themselves empowered these women:

Katrina loved politics and had since she was in student government in high school. In college, she had majored in Liberal Arts because she thought that going into politics was off-putting because her ex-boyfriend had told her that women in politics were all upset that they didn't have a penis. This comment stayed with her. Yet, a decade after college graduation she was still jazzed up anytime she had a political conversation. At the urging of a friend, she decided that she no longer was going to hide her passion of politics and got a small job on a campaign trail where she had the opportunity to do public relations work. When the campaign ended, she was so sparked that she opened her own PR company that specialized in political topics.

***

Genelle was beyond embarrassed that every week she went to help support teenaged girls who had experienced abortion. Her family was completely pro-choice and Genelle felt like she could never tell. Years after helping a suffering teen, the teen found her and thanked her for being there for her when no one else was and asked Genelle to speak on a panel supporting women's rights. Genelle almost said no but decided to employ the bravery of her New You and said yes. She now runs an organization that helps at-risk youth.

What about the thoughts or truths that the New You has that don't work out so well? Maybe they don't seem popular. Girl, I have heard those too. It's okay to believe and think what you believe and think. What is no longer okay is pretending that you don't feel the way you do to have your root feeling met. The New You does not hide who she is to please the masses. She also doesn't have to be unkind with her beliefs.

As you get to know the New You, take an honest look at your hidden thoughts. It's important to spell these out so that they don't become secrets.

1. What do you feel is off-putting or obnoxious about you?

2. What are your most unpopular thoughts/beliefs?

3. What opinions do you keep to yourself?

Here's a few women who had hidden ideas on very hot topics:

Sheba believes that there are only two sexes, male and female. She isn't buying that there are sixty-four terms or more to describe gender. She also thinks that sexuality and gender confusion are a fad. What she doesn't do is show unkindness to others with different beliefs.

***

Kathy hates 12-step programs. She thinks they are a cult. She is embarrassed that she feels this way but she does.

***

Sabrina would be horrified if anyone knew that she voted for Donald Trump twice. She did and she likes him and his daughters and doesn't think he is a bad person.

When you begin to live in alignment, you are living in your power. We've all seen people who seem to have it going on. They know what to do, what to say, and command a room in an easy way that makes you want to buy whatever it is that they are selling. They have an ease and a flow of confidence that exudes from their being. These people have learned something important. Their values. Living in their values they are no longer pretending to be something that they're not. They aren't being jerks about what they stand for. They live an unapologetic lifestyle that doesn't harm others, especially themselves. They live lives full of purpose, power, and potential because they have done enough self-discovery and honest assessment to live in and discover their highest values.

Values are the guiding principles that give our lives meaning and a roadmap on how to prioritize what we say yes to, who we spend time with, where we invest our financial, emotional, and physical resources. When you know what you value as the New You, life gets easier and there is no drive to make secrets. You are no longer swayed by the Old

You and her people-pleasing, root feeling chasing ways. Remember that nice guy that you dated but it was a disaster? Different values. Remember that job that you tolerated but the money was good? Out of alignment. How about the time you said yes when you meant no and were seething about it for weeks and created secrets because of it? Yup, not in your values.

When you are out of alignment, you are out of integrity, and by default you create secrets. The Old You didn't always use her value system but the New You lives in alignment and stays within the safety of her values. Knowing what you value simplifies chaos. It's like a magic wand cutting through the bull. Knowing what you value is a new tool you can grab when you don't know what to reach for because it will aid you in not taking things personally. It's the personalization that led to so many of our secrets to begin with. Think about it, I took it personally when my husband left me in the church, and that created a violent secret. Think of your secret, what did you take personally that led to being a secret?

We create stories and keep secrets about being in relationships with people who have values contrary to our way of being and our value system. We don't always know that it's our values that are in conflict and we make it a bigger issue by taking it personally and giving it a storyline. People create high drama with their stories when they don't have to be that big. You can value something that a person you're in a relationship with doesn't and it can still be harmonious. Or, you can decide that there is too much spiritual sandpaper and that it isn't a good fit for you.

Here are some examples of values that women shared:

Tanya's boss was always gruff with her when she met with him. She thought she was doing a good job of giving an overview of all that was happening in her department. Her boss however always sighed and seemed agitated. Come to find out Tanya valued being thorough and detailed, but her boss valued time, being precise, and getting to the bottom line.

***

Carla and her husband got along great in almost every aspect of their relationship, The sandpaper between them always showed up with being on time. Carla was someone who was ready early and wanted to arrive early. She valued being a person of her word and the gift of time. Her husband valued being a free spirit, not stressing, and going with the flow. Their main fight always played out with Carla feeling disrespected and her husband feeling like she was uptight.

Learning how to communicate your values will help you to live in the New You, without creating drama or secrets. When you know your values and the values of others, you can create powerful interactions that you do not leave the tinge of resentment of secret-keeping in their wake. Realizing the power of values releases you from keeping secrets. Values are personal and become motivators and guideposts for the New You.

Part 3: Define Your Highest Values

Tools like step-by-step guides, worksheets, and personality tests are available online and in many coaching books to determine your personal values. My favorite way to help people find their values takes a different approach and should help you to get to the heart of what you value quickly. Don't overthink it; feel it.

1. Write down a list of Pet Peeves. What irks you or gets under your skin? What upsets you?

2. Flip your list to see what you value.

Here are some examples to help:

Sheila hated when her boss was condescending to her co-worker. Sheila valued equality.

***

Liz could not stand it when her husband said he would do something and then didn't follow through. Liz valued integrity.

***

Naomi hated when people skated through life without doing their part. She valued contribution.

Maybe you can't stand it when people are late. Your value is punctuality, but ultimately, you want your time to be respected. If you are annoyed by pessimistic people who don't move forward, your value is optimism and action. If you hate it when people are phony bologna or only talk about shallow topics, you value authenticity and connection. Once you've defined your values, post your top five where you can see them and use them as guideposts to living fully in the life of the New You. When you have to make a decision and you can feel the pull of the Old You, ask the question, *What's my highest value?* This will ward off the ways of the Old You while letting the New You choose what action to take next.

One word of caution: you may find yourself omitting or embellishing to justify your new values because of insecurity. Just because you are operating in your new values does not make you bulletproof to secrets. Keep an eye out for some of the lead-up signs that you may backslide to false self-behavior. Fearing you are not perfect, guilt about your opinion, saying yes when you mean no, people-pleasing, or bullying are all indicators you may feel you have to coerce an outcome . . . and create a secret.

Three tips to not create new value secrets:

1. Do a body check. If you've had an interaction and feel sick to your stomach, tense, nervous, or agitated, you are probably blurring your values and are on the verge of creating a secret that will go against them. Use your body for clues to see if you are out of alignment.

2. Post your values where you can see them. When you don't know what to do ask yourself, what is my highest value? Take action on that and remind yourself of what your life was like when you were collecting secrets.

3. Your values are a way of life. Be willing to walk away from people and situations that might pull you into the Old You.

Look to these examples of how to stay in your value system:

Shrivanti was newly sober. When she would go out with her friends from her party days she was always tempted to backslide and drink. Her highest value was living in full consciousness. She had to make a choice to not go out with these friends anymore because she was out of alignment with her New You.

***

Lisa's stomach would hurt whenever she was overworked. Her highest value was her family and in the New You she had made her children and spouse a priority. Anytime she worked past six she inevitably didn't feel well. She used the body sensation as a reminder to clock out for the day so that she could live in her value system.

***

In the beginning, Colleen had a hard time making decisions in the New You. She kept her values as wallpaper on her computer screen. Whenever anyone asked her for something she would check it against her values and ask herself if what she was about to say yes to was in alignment with her New You.

 Realizing the power of values releases you from keeping secrets.

Learning to live in your values requires diligence and is paramount to completing Stage Nine in the Secret-Breaking System. But in the end, it makes life much easier to cut through because you are no longer taking on obligations or engaging in relationships that are not in alignment with your highest values. You have built the foundation of the New You and you don't want to create secrets or lies with her.

Life becomes easier to navigate when you are living in alignment because we are no longer willing to prioritize the energetic and requested obligations that come our way. In other words, you are going to simply say yes or no and mean it.

Energetically, spiritually, and emotionally you will be protecting the time and space of the New You. If you say yes to one obligation and then to another, and then another, you will stack up so many yeses that you will not have time to dedicate to your own life.

To stay in alignment, we also must get clear on what are and are not willing to do. We've all heard of the *to-do* list where you keep a list of your tasks that need to get done. The *to-do* list is about setting an intention to complete the tasks at hand, and it can be a powerful tool to move forward. The *"I WON'T"* list is equally as powerful. An *"I WON'T"* list consists of the open loops in your life that are draining your energy and keeping you from New You living. They are the negotiations you make with yourself that you have no desire to take action on but feel bad or guilty for not doing. They are the items on your to-do list that have been on there for months with no action taken. They take up time and emotional energy because they live in the back of your mind and poke at you giving you a little jolt of adrenaline that can lead to secret-keeping. The worst part about open loops is the story the critical narrator of the Old You creates because it is in conflict with the New You. The New You knows what she wants and also knows that she does not intend to spend time on completing the tasks, hopes, and dreams of the Old You. Closing the loops the Old You created will stop the energy drain and make space for more purposeful New You activities.

My personal *"I WON'T"* list consists of making recipes that take more than thirty minutes, washing my car (my husband can do that), cleaning out the garage, saying yes to virtual speaking gigs where I have to share the event with at least 5,000 people on my email list, and printing out the thousands of photos I have of my family and creating scrapbooks. Those are the small ones. The Old You would say, *good moms spend a lot of time cooking, they make scrapbooks, they keep the garage organized.* My New You didn't believe that. She already understood that I was a good mom and that my time was better spent being present with my children rather than trying to catalog and capture past moments with a camera.

Closing loops has power, keeps you in alignment with the New You, and ushers out the ways of Old You and her critical narrator.

> *Kendra was in trouble with the IRS and they were going to take money out of her bank accounts, she was able to admit that it was because she never filed the paperwork or looked at her checkbook. She had no idea how much she owed and felt guilty because she had been told that she had a math brain her entire life. When she put IRS filings and banking on her "I WON'T" list, it opened her up to hire an accountant who took care of her banking for her. It freed up at least eight hours for her a month because she had spent that amount of time thinking about what she should be doing and worrying. Now she uses those eight hours at Toastmaster's, working on her public speaking to further her career. Her Old You would have her feel guilty and would tell her that she wasn't smart and that only irresponsible people got in trouble with the IRS. Her New You was softer and gentler and understood that she valued asking for help.*

Creating an "I WON'T" list is invigorating and powerful and will make saying no even easier.

Part 4: Create Your "I WON'T LIST"

1. List your open loops. They might be business deals you toy with, men you think about dating, exes you fantasize about getting back together with, tasks that you feel obligated to do, projects that are shiny, hiring a coach, and so on.

2. Circle any that are full-body, hell yeses that you are certain the New You wants to take action on.

3. Based on the values of the New You, create an I Won't list from the open loops of anything that is not a hell yes—therefore, closing the loop. These can be things like going back to school to get a master's degree, volunteering, cleaning underneath your bed, networking with people from high school, or partnering with that person who has an interesting idea that you have very little desire to do.

 Closing loops has power, keeps you in alignment with the New You, and ushers out the ways of Old You and her critical narrator.

As you're building your New You, you will want ammunition to continue with your changes. Noticing your positive effect on people will allow your subconscious to release the Old You and its narrative about who you used to be. If you turned just a quarter of your negative thoughts about who you are into positive praise, your entire life would change. That change in you will create a change in others. They will no longer be locked in the same dance steps with you because your dance steps are different. Your shift will cause a shift. That is purpose, power, and potential.

We can't always see our attributes, but others can, and we need to pay attention to what they say because it can be a powerful indicator of who we are. My clients describe me as powerful, on point, intuitive, bright, caring, loving, on it, skillful, leader, kind, masterful, guide, and wise. I pay attention when I receive feedback. Occasionally a new descriptor will be added. Funny was one that I loved.

Part 5: Notice What Others Notice About You

Don't be shy. Let's flaunt what you've got. The key to this exercise is to start noticing your impact.

1. What are the positive things that people say about you? Start keeping an ongoing list so that you can see how you show up in the world.

2. Write down the ways that you have helped others and created a positive impact.

3. Read it daily. End it with, "who you are makes a difference."

As you say goodbye to the Old You, you will begin to unlock the truest parts of your core. Your New You will lead you to unexpected paths and reveal untapped dreams. But what happens when you are faced with a situation where it's tempting to pick up old behaviors and secret-keeping patterns? How do you deal with people who insist on treating you like you are the Old You? They see and hear your new behavior, but they knew you when . . . and you find that no matter how much you try, whenever they see you, they meet you with the "wink wink" of knowing who you used to be. They haven't changed and want to pull you back into the old way of living with lower thinking and shiny objects. This is sometimes the hardest part of becoming the New You.

I was at a gathering with a girlfriend of mine and an old friend from the past was there with her husband. She lost her temper and threw her drink at him and stomped away, pulling me with her as she stormed out. She went on a five-minute tirade of what an ass her husband was and said she knew I would understand. You see, she had been at a sorority function decades before and had seen me throw a drink in my boyfriend's face. That version of me was long-gone and even though I knew she had been a part of me, it had been so long since I had acted that way, that it was almost foreign to me. Instead of condoning her behavior, I asked her what she needed. She was caught off guard and said, "Are you f-ing kidding me? Unbelievable," and walked back into the party.

Not everyone is going to like your changes or believe that they're real. The longer you live in the New You, the more believable you will be to others and yourself. To start living in this new, secret-free world will take trust in yourself and practice. To do this, you will need to prepare yourself with new tools that will strengthen your new way of being. At first, you may feel like you are continuously working Stage Nine in the Secret Breaking System until one day you realize it's been weeks since you fell back into old behavior or created new secrets. I assure you this experience will happen if you commit 100 percent to live in your New You. And I promise, you are going to like what you see. She is awesome!

Dirty Little Deep Dives

1. You have purpose, power, and potential.

2. Commit 100 percent to the New You and say goodbye to the Old You.

3. Contrary action is your go-to tool.

4. Who you are makes a difference.

STAGE TEN

Creating Your Ripple Effect

Sister, you have been thorough, honest, and forthcoming, taking the many twists and turns during our journey together through your one dark and pressing secret. In this time of deep self-reflection, you gave yourself a great gift that many women never receive: understanding, honoring, and revealing all the ways you came to be who you are today. You've looked your false self in the eye, thanked her, and bid her farewell while inviting the New You and your truest self to the party of life. Season one of your time on this planet is over and season two is launching with a better cast, better wardrobe, a bigger budget, and a better script.

We have arrived at the tenth and final stage in the Secret-Breaking System: Creating Your Ripple Effect. What is a ripple effect? It's the New You taking all that has been revealed to you about yourself and walking your new talk to inspire other women to stop hiding behind their secrets. Your ripple effect is you stepping into your purpose and bigger living.

It's the impact you create in the world around you with your secret-free actions, interactions, behaviors, and thoughts. It's the everlasting impression you leave behind and the announcement of self that you bring forward. When you walk into a room as the New You, confident and collected, other women can't help but notice and be attracted to what you're emulating. Not in an egocentric way, but in a way that is magnetic and draws others in. Your allure and appeal coupled with your authenticity, and self-assured nature will have them take notice and wonder, *what does she know that I don't*. The New You is eager to help the woman still suffering, rid herself of the burden of her secrets, and in so doing, the work of helping secret keepers begins. Having shed your troublesome and shameful past this New You is available to create opportunities that open you up to give and receive. In the Old You, most of us were takers or we over gave in to survive. Now we are right-sized givers and love others and ourselves, knowing that this kind of love poses no threat, takes nothing from us, and grows.

You are in a very small percentage of women willing to dig deep to let go of the shame of their secrets. Now the burden and the privilege of sharing what you've learned in this 10-Stage Secret-Breaking System belongs to you. It's time to pass the baton to another woman and pull her out of the ashes. You, my friend, are the ripples in the pond. And ladies, the pond is huge.

Here's what comes next. You've found the golden gem of your true self, the New You, through the secret you've taken through the system. It's important that you do not stop there. To continue your growth you must go back through the 10-Stage Secret-Breaking System with all of your secrets and any future secret you create (yes, we are human after all). Each secret left in the dust empowers you to do more for others because you have opened space in your life and stepped into new ways of being and thinking. The false self is begging to get back in with her time-consuming and costly survival tools. Stay vigilant and continue to bring the New You into the light. Lean into your faith and think about the women you can champion with the experiences you can share about what happened for you when you told your secrets. You have purposeful service work to do and must be determined to be committed to the process of giving back.

Here's something else to consider, your ripple is all of who you are. The positive and the negative. Those positive attributes that you wrote down and have been referring to in Stage Nine, are the proudest parts of your ripple effect. So are the attributes you didn't write down. The negative ones. Your way of being is contagious and reflects what is going on for you internally. That internal indicator spills over and touches others. This is important and the New You must consider the power her vibe puts out. Your emotional, physical, mental, and spiritual state must be a top priority to create an intentional ripple that you are proud of because you are creating a ripple regardless. Every day, the way you show up seeps out and onto others. Wherever you go, you create a ripple. When you're alone, your mood and thoughts create a ripple for you. When you are out, those same thoughts determine your behavior and create a ripple. Intentional ripple creation is the responsibility that the New You is faced with. And I have to tell you, learning how to put out a contagious ripple that you are proud of is empowering.

Think about the times that you've been in a good mood, had high energy, and were authentically fun to be around. People around you are lifted by that energy because energy is contagious. You leave them feeling better than when you came in. Your interaction with the next person charged them up. It feels good to provide this kind of expansive energy, hence creating a ripple. You say hi to the grocer, put down your phone, and sincerely ask about their day, that's a ripple. You take your shopping cart back to the cart stand, ripple. You let your sister leave her kids at your house for the weekend so that she can reconnect with her husband, ripple.

The same is true when you're in a bad mood, agitated, scared, or anxiety-ridden. You might come home and bring that mood to your spouse or partner. They feel your agitation. Suddenly their good mood is gone (unless they have rock-solid boundaries) and you have brought restrictive energy to the relationship, hence creating a tsunami. Maybe you're driving and lost in the negative thoughts your mind presents you with and are fantasizing about a worst-case scenario and another driver tries to merge over and you give him the finger, ripple. Or you are in the car yelling at your kids and someone notices and calls you on it and you tell them to mind their own business, ripple.

High or low, positive or negative, good or bad, you are creating ripples with every single thought you think and action you take. The New You cares about the wake she creates. She is mindful of her inner narrative because she knows that her false self is waiting in the curtain, eager to tempt her into creating secrets.

I'm not saying to make yourself a martyr to others and their feelings. Hell no. You have every right to feel your feelings. But you also have a responsibility to your New You. We can fall back into old traps of thinking negatively because we were wired on the defense for so long. So, when you want to be in a bad mood, or complain, or not be of assistance, look at how it's limiting your life and affecting others.

Mary was constantly tired and whenever she ran into anyone, and they would ask how she was, she would always lead with how tired she was. One day she was out to lunch with her BFF and began telling her how tired she was. The friend said, "I wonder what you would do in your life if you weren't always so tired?" Mary took notice. Even though the comment hurt her feelings, she knew her friend was right. She started going to bed earlier and exercising to have more energy.

***

Zoe was naturally happy, and people always included her in their plans. She loved being a part of and when people would ask her what her secret was, she told them she made sure to write a gratitude list daily and that she didn't say yes to plans that didn't energize her.

***

Stacey was intimidating and people were scared to approach her. She wanted to have more friends and opportunities but didn't know how. One day she decided that she would smile and make eye contact with everyone she encountered. She noticed that people responded to her with more enthusiasm, and she was even asked out on a date.

Part 1: Noticing Your Ripple

It's so easy to go into auto-pilot, check-out, multi-task and go fast. For the next week, you are going to intentionally pay attention to the ripple you create and notice how others respond:

1. Take note of your interactions with everyone you encounter from the mailman, the repairman, the grocer, your cleaning lady, your kids, friends, parents, husband, co-workers, and neighbors. How do behave with them? What response do you get in return?

2. Pick a day and be intentional about saying hello to everyone you encounter with a smile on your face. Thoughtfully send them good feelings as you interact or pass by them. Make eye contact wherever possible. Note your ripple.

3. Notice your energy levels and keep a journal to write down the difference in your interactions when your energy level was high versus low.

4. Pay attention to your low or agitated energy and notice the difference in how others respond to you and the feeling left in the room versus when your energy is fueled with positivity.

5. What is your go-to energy feeling? Example, dread, excitement, optimism, love, agitation, anxiety. Knowing what feeling you are predisposed to is a key to shifting your energy to create a different ripple.

 You are the ripples in the pond.

Many secret-keepers need a big dose of self-love. We need to pay attention to the way we treat ourselves, the attitude we have toward ourselves, and the mean thoughts we have about ourselves. Our actions, attitudes, and disdain for who we are, are not conducive to creating powerful ripples. We look in the mirror and judge ourselves harshly. We rush around eager to accomplish, overdo it, and feel burnt out. Then we beat ourselves up for not doing more. We treat ourselves like robots and lash ourselves with our thoughts.

In the New You, we let go of our unkind and abusive behavior toward ourselves and step into the highest percentage of our true selves. No more 50/50 split with the false self. We should be in 90 percent true self by the time we run a handful of secrets through the Secret-Breaking System. To sustain that state, we have to put ourselves first on our list. It is imperative that we take the closed loops from the I Won'ts and our values from Stage Nine and covet our time to do good in the world our way. We will now fill that time with self-care, purposeful work, dreams, goals, and our aspirations for life.

For many of us, self-care was always last on our list of priorities, or it sounded frivolous or like a time-waster. Self-care may have been synonymous with getting a massage or a manicure, and while that kind of self-care is important, I want you to look deeper so that you don't fall back into the gutter of life. When we show care for ourselves, we fill our own cup and root feeling. We no longer need to chase after bad relationships or take secret actions because when the New You leads with her true self, she is no longer desperate to chase her feelings. She learned how to be this way by taking care of herself spiritually, emotionally, mentally, and physically. No longer putting the needs of the false self of other people before her own, she makes herself a daily priority so that she can give from a full cup. The New You has decided to live in a bigger container and knows that to do that, there are no quick fixes. Her new way of being is a way of life and will require more than a quarterly massage to maintain. To look outward and to be of service, you must look inward and take care of you first.

Part 2: Finding Your Oxygen Mask

Like a passenger on a plane, to help anyone else, you have to put on your own oxygen mask first. Answer the following questions to help you define how you will get your oxygen.

1. What kind of emotional and mental support do you need on an ongoing basis so that you don't slide backward and create more secrets? Example: support group, therapist, coach, the 12-Step Program, or an accountability partner.

2. What do you do for physical fitness and how often?

3. What daily practice will help you to start your day on solid footing?

4. How can you connect to Your God more often?

5. What professionals do you need to see for self-care? Examples: doctor for a checkup, mammogram, dentist, chiropractor, acupuncturist, and so on.

6. What fills your tank that feels indulgent? Examples: massage, nails, girls' trips, workshops.

7. What do you do for fun?

8. What do you do for self-development?

The days of you playing second fiddle are over. It's time to be in your own spotlight so you can help others. As you look at your answers, consider what needs to be adjusted on this list so that you can take good care of yourself because your ripple effect is the undercurrent of who you are. It precedes and follows you affecting all that it encounters.

You've done an immeasurable amount of work. Yes, calling out one secret through the system deserves a standing ovation. You identified the secret, defined its one-two-three punch, and put a microscope on the narrative of your false self. You evaluated how your false self was created and named your faulty wiring while discovering your tripwire emotion. You defined your root feeling and how living a life of secrets has been costing you in all areas of your life. You faced your false self and questioned your good enough living while looking at your patterns and your shadow behaviors. As hard or uncomfortable as it may have been, you defined meaning for Your God and looked at faith. You prepared to tell your secret, took a risk assessment, and then told. You bravely challenged your limiting beliefs, granted forgiveness, took note of what might cause you to keep more secrets, and made a commitment to let go of that behavior by saying goodbye to the Old You once and for all. You've made a steadfast choice to go back through the system on each and every secret you've kept so that you can live in a bigger container and create an intentional ripple.

Girl, you are immense!

Now take what you know to the streets and give back to the women in your world who you know are confused and still holding on to a life that no longer serves them. Hold their hand as they walk through the Secret-Breaking System. Tell them to stop with the secrets.

The gifts you've received from this process have been many and will bloom and multiply over time. To get the full impact, you must share what you know. When the proverbial gong sounds and another woman is intrigued by your ripple or is still outwardly hurting, that is your cue to share what you know. The magic of Stage Ten is that your once shameful story is made whole and becomes an actual life-changing miracle for someone else. To create the miracle, you have to share it.

So, few women have taken the call and invitation to deeply discover who they are. Any woman can do this Secret-Breaking System. We can all be secret breakers but as you've learned, the process requires time, introspection, and faith, but never as much time as you have spent burying who you truly were in a life you were not happy leading.

You are a phenomenal woman even if you don't think so. I am here to tell you that by reading this whole book, even if you only did half the work, you are already on your way to the next level of your life. Your secret is part of your story. Let the impact of your story on other women too scared to share encourage you to do all the work. When you share your secret you not only free yourself, but you lift someone else who needs to hear what you have to say so that they can experience a moment where the light of hope turns on.

 When we show care for ourselves, we fill our own cup and root feeling.

I have shared my secret of violence more times than I can count. And always, every time, there is at least one woman who will come up to me and tell me that she has been violent as well and because of my honesty, she feels hope. And that ladies, is the door we need to kick through. It's the invitation we need to give. It's one of hope. It's the belief that if you can be different—*if I can be different*—she can be different. We are all the same at our core—guts and DNA. What works for one, can work for another. We have to link arms and share the truth and break the stigma that we are alone and should be ashamed. Every single woman has a story to tell. Each one of us can use it to create a ripple in the world.

American poet, civil rights activist, and author of "I Know Why the Caged Bird Sings," Maya Angelou, was a sex worker and madam (female pimp) when she was a struggling mother. She was no different than you or I except she decided to share what she knew and her work, filled with her heartbreak and her secrets, became a legacy that freed so many and gave them the space and the courage to live bigger.

***

Stacey Green, normal, run-of-the-mill, average woman, was using suboxone to kick her heroin habit when she was pregnant with her first child. Now, she is clean and sober and helps other women release their shame and judgment of themselves due to their drug addiction. If she wouldn't have been willing to share her darkest hour with others, they might still be in theirs.

***

Michelle Obama went to marriage counseling with President Barack Obama. The First Lady struggled with her weight and gained thirty pounds while she was in office. She took that experience and created a weight program to help others get in shape.

And can we talk about Oprah for a minute? Even Oprah, hands down one of the most successful and influential women in the world, has shared about being molested, using drugs, and losing a baby from a teenage pregnancy at fourteen. Her candor, openness, and honesty have left an imprint on millions.

 Your once shameful story is made whole and becomes an actual life-changing miracle for someone else.

Sharing your truth with another woman will give her the courage and curiosity to explore living secret-free. What women need is the moment of understanding where we don't feel alone. And while all of us can't be Oprah, we all have our own platform of people to share with. Never underestimate the power of sharing with just one. The one right in front of you. The one who needs a hug. The one who when you ask her how she is, stifles the tears. The one who needs to be listened to.

While some of us might write our truths through a blog or a book, or podcast and speak on stages, others of us might share more quietly. All of it makes a difference, one sharing of a secret at a time. Wherever you share and however you share is less important than the sharing itself. You are listening for the opportunity to speak life into someone else. If a woman hints she is feeling lousy, you can share that you've been there too. If a woman is outwardly upset, you can take her hand and lend an ear. If a woman is angry, mean, or intimidating, you can pray for the moment to be able to share a piece of your past that will help her to break free from her future. Listening is the key to sharing your secret. It may be a piece, or it may be all of it. The entire #MeToo movement was created because one woman shared, another woman believed her, and another shared. And on and on it went. The world took notice and changes were made. Women want to link arms. They want to stand together and be understood but someone has to go first. That someone is you.

Remember the mantra in Stage Nine? I have purpose, power, and potential. Leading with your purpose to serve another woman will allow you to live fully awake and to take a position of leadership over your own life instead of one of reactivity. Any victimhood that you subscribed to as a secret-keeper will not serve you in this new purpose-driven life. Your New You will require you to be authentically who you are. Any desire to compare yourself to others will set you back. You do not have to be a superstar or celebrity to create your ripple effect. You can be exactly who you are. We are all meant to create change in the world we live in. Make the decision to courageously create change in yours.

Hopefully, you are reading this stage and saying, Gretchen, *I drank the Kool-Aid. I am on board with my true self! No more triggers holding me back! I am on fire.* Dear one, I love your intention but there is a real risk of that flame going out if you do not make a firm commitment to the New You. While intentionality is a wonderful tool to use in your life, you must have firm commitments to support them or else they blow away and become a promising idea that you used to think about or worse, another open loop that can lead to secret-keeping. To ensure follow-through, you must take your intentions from being "airy-fairy" and make them concrete. What are you actually going to do? When will you do it? How will you do it? You must know these answers. When we make a full decision to lean in, our intentions built on commitment become the actions that we take that create our ripple effect.

As we near the end of our journey, you have a choice to make about the way your life is going to play out from here. If you keep doing what you've always done you will live a life that is much the same as it is today. Because that is your default. But, if you decide to live a life built from committed action, your life will change. In order to do this, you must get serious about the ripple effect you want to create in your own life secret-free by committing to what fills you up.

Part 3: A Life of Action

Close your eyes and imagine two years into the future.

- Where do you live?

- What risk did you take to make your life of an intention a life of commitment?

- What dream are you living?

- Are you in a community of action?

- Who do you serve?

- What makes you most proud?

- Are you feeling loved by those around you?

- Who is your biggest support?

- What feelings do you experience the most often?

- What ripple are you creating?

- What action will you take today to support this future?

Reflect on your answers. In order to pull your future into the present, what intention do you need to create and partner with committed action?

 Our intentions built on commitment become the actions that we take that create our ripple effect.

Standing in your New You, it's important to claim the life you are committed to living. I want you to imagine lassoing your future life and pulling it into today. We've lived on default for so long, but the New You lives bigger and creates what she wants and takes the actions to get there. Your committed life is where you will find the women that you are supposed to help. As we stand in the New You, we are fulfilling our hidden dreams and living in purpose. The people we are supposed to touch with our ripple are waiting for us there.

Your secrets, that once bound you, will become one of your greatest assets as you share them with the women that you attract. They no longer hold the sting of the past because you have worked through the mire and the muck and have left your old ways behind. You are no longer embarrassed about who you used to be or the secrets that you've kept because they have lost their grip in your life. When you share your secret action story, it has no emotional charge. It's just the facts of what life used to look like. Nothing more and nothing less.

My story about the stabbing is neutral today. The untangling of the secret showed me that I never stabbed my husband. I did feel violent. I did chase him. I did raise the key. But the stabbing was a product of my false self's critical narrator and was used to keep me small and to keep me from creating a positive and powerful ripple. I lived under the shame of the embellishment and my false self kept me living on the sidelines of life.

I'll never forget the day a former secret-keeper changed my life forever and was the catalyst to me deciding to embark on my journey to live secret-free. In an intimate moment when I was deep in the pain of my secret, she told a long ago released secret of her own. She shared that on a night many years before, her husband had passed out drunk, in their front yard in a pile of leaves. Her faulty wiring had been activated and she lit a cigar, put it in his mouth, and hoped that the leaves would catch on fire (they didn't). She told her story from a place of detachment and without shame. She spoke of the hope that came from living secret-free in her New You. Had I not heard her secret, I may never have known that a new way of being was waiting for me. I might have missed my great big life and my purpose, and the writing of this book. I will be forever grateful to her for sharing her secret. I know that someone will be forever grateful to you for you sharing yours.

When I go to speak, people who know the story of the "stabbing" ask that I share it. I always include it, to remember who I was, to see how much I've grown, and to help the woman still struggling. Each and every time I tell this story, a woman will come up to me and share a struggle of her own. I've had a woman tell me that she slashed her husband's tires. I had another tell me that she tackled her husband and bit his leg in the front yard while their neighbors watched because she was out of her mind with rage.

On and on the secrets spill. Much like the woman who shared her secret with me, when I tell my story now, I have no attachment. The woman telling it today is much different than the woman who lived it. That's the gift of living secret-free. When the charge of the secrets is gone, hope gives life to others.

While you were reading this book and doing the work, you changed. You may see some results already. I promise that as you continue to live secret-free there is a bigger life waiting for you. You need to create the ripple by being in the intentionality of action and by committing to your purpose of service. You know those women we see who seem to say it like it is but without anger and not particularly upsetting anybody, and they appear to be so complete in their skin? Go look in the mirror babe and have a chat with yourself. You already are that woman and the more that you know this truth, the more you will lean this way.

Our secrets have made us resilient and that is a gift. Use your gift. Share your secret and your change as your ripple effect. We are no longer slaves to our shame or our secrets. You are a new creation. You were set apart for a special purpose. Your story is powerful. Use it, tell it, forgive yourself. Honor your secrets. Each secret got you to this exact moment where you became the woman who wanted more and decided to do the work to get it.

As you move forward always keep this question in mind, *Will my New You be grateful for the decisions I'm making today, or will they lead to more secret-keeping?* With your most honest answer, go out and design the life you deserve full of love, peace, joy, and service. The rewards of this new way of living have only just begun. Your best days are ahead of you waiting for you to step in and claim them and to take your rightful place. With all that you have learned and all that you have shed, this new way of living stands before you and is within reach of your grasp. It's time to open your hands and your heart and let that new way of being seep through you from the top of your head to the tip of your toes, knowing that you are now partnered with your New You and that your secret was always the miracle underneath.

Dirty Little Deep Dives

1. Self-care is the cornerstone to living as the New You

2. Every intention needs a commitment and an action.

3. Sharing your secret is a beacon of hope that will free another woman.

4. Your secret is a lifesaving gift to you and to others. It's the miracle underneath.

DIRTY LITTLE SECRETS – 60 UNCENSORED SECRETS

The secrets listed below range in shock value and subject matter, in no particular order to show the chaos of secret-keeping in a woman's life. What every one of these women from all parts of the world share is their shame and how the secrets weaponize them against themselves. Sister, you are never alone. Animal, vegetable, or fruit—it's all been done. I hope you get a good chuckle from one or more of these secrets. We need to acknowledge our insanity to survive and, through our transparency, heal. I hope you read this list and think, *I'm not that bad after all* and maybe even have an *OMG* moment or two. But understand, regardless of the depth of our secrets, if we hold them, we are not set free.

- I opened a credit card in my roommate's name and maxed out the card.

- I had sex with my daughter's eighteen-year-old boyfriend after I got him drunk.

- I gave my boyfriend's dad a blow job.

- I embezzled thousands of dollars from a company I worked for.

- I am on antidepressants and don't want anyone to know.

- For decades, I've lied and told people I have a master's degree, but I don't.

- One night I was so horny that I used an eggplant to penetrate myself.

- I put tuna juice on my clit and let my cat lick it.

- I can see why people put vodka in baby bottles and was tempted to do the same thing.

- I tried to have sex with my massage therapist and when he turned me down, I turned him for sexual harassment.

- I've been in a porno that went viral on Pornhub. It has ruined my life. I am a professional and had to quit my job because of it.

- My teenage daughter is a jerk. I cannot stand her and do not know how I produced this child.

- I had terrible postpartum but didn't know what it was. I robotically did what I was supposed to with my newborn but dreaded it. I cried every night and wondered if this was how it would always be. I felt tricked into parenting and desperately wanted my old life back. I felt ashamed for how much I disliked being a mom. It was so much harder than I'd expected. When other women would talk about how much they loved it, I would nod and say that I did too. I was filled with shame that I didn't feel differently and thought that something was inherently wrong with me.

- I don't know how to control my kids. We don't spank, but I want to. I do pinch them, and I've grabbed them too hard.

- I was jealous of my roommate and wanted her life. When people would call the house I would pretend to be her. I slept with her boyfriend knowing that I had herpes and hoped that I gave it to her.

- I slept with my roommate's boyfriend and when her friends would call, I would pretend I was her and say terrible things.

- I stole my best friend's parents' checkbook and forged their name across the country to the tune of ten thousand dollars.

- I called the receptionist in my doctor's office a bitch because I thought she was condescending.

- I am terrified all the time that I am messing my kids up. I worry that they will hate me when they grow up.

- I don't want to look up my kids' school updates online. I don't care and wish they would just forge my name.

- Being a mom is overrated. People talk about it being the best thing that happens to you. I seriously do not feel this way. I can't stand my children.

- I smoked weed with my daughter when she was thirteen. I still smoke it with her and tell myself it's okay because weed is legal. I feel shame about it.

- I think that Democrats are babies and that people should fend for themselves.

- My parents can never find out that my sister is gay. They will kick her out of the family, and then she will hate me, and I will never see her again.

- I stole my co-worker's food from the fridge day in and day out. Every time he would ask who took it, I would act like I didn't know.

- When I was a hostess, I stole the tips from the tables that were left for the wait staff. I did most of the work and they never shared their split with me. I would skim a buck here and a buck there.

- I found out that my kids are watching porn. I feel so ashamed. I feel scared. I don't know how to help them or what to do. I feel like I've failed them somehow. I feel like I wasn't diligent enough to keep them from finding it or looking.

- My son got a girlfriend and now I feel like I am in the middle of a breakup. It's the strangest thing to be "replaced" by another woman. I know it's not logical, but I am overwhelmingly sad.

- When I was a babysitter, I would put the kids in front of the TV and invited my boyfriend over and went into the master bedroom to have sex with him since we didn't have anywhere else to do it.

- My vagina smells. I don't know who in the heck is ever going to go downtown. I don't have an infection. I've been checked out by the "gyno" many times. It's just my natural odor, and I am so embarrassed by it.

- I was obsessed with food and would buy it and throw it away. One night, I cooked lasagna and the glass pan exploded. I waited for it to cool down and picked out the glass pieces and ate it anyway.

- My baby cried and cried and cried. I couldn't stand it or her. I wanted out. I wanted to leave him or put him up for adoption. It was maddening. I feel terrible admitting this.

- In the third grade, a kid was so mean to my son. He was bullying him daily. I confronted the kid and told him to knock it off and that I would wait for him every day after school to make sure that he was behaving.

- I had an affair with my best friend's husband when my kids were little. I used to go to their house for play dates and have photos of all of us together. This went on for three years while I was married to my addict/alcoholic spouse.

- At the height of my drug addiction, my father was diagnosed and became terminally ill with bone cancer. While on his last week of life, I had stolen the remaining cash he had in his nightstand and spent the next three days chasing a cocaine high.

- I used to make my husband pay me for sex. He had to put money in a jar before I would sleep with him. He had so much money and I didn't work, and I felt like he owed it to me.

- I would never want my boss to know that when I was in my twenties, I danced for Coyote Ugly in Las Vegas. I am sure he would view me differently, and I have worked so hard to get to where I am.

- I pee when I laugh. I pee when I run. I've peed in the bushes of someone's house when I was out for a walk because I was too far from home to make it and there was no bathroom in sight.

- I'm a high-paid escort with enough money to live in a house near the beach. Every time I realize that I'm a prostitute, I feel a little ashamed. The money is so good that it's hard to stop. Both of my kids have different fathers who paid me to have sex with them.

- I jumped out of a moving car on the freeway because I was so enraged with my boyfriend. Then I picked up rocks and threw them at his car as he kept driving. When the police were called, I told them that he pushed me out, and he got arrested.

- My daughter used to cry so much at night when she was little that I started giving her Tylenol to make her sleep. One night, it wasn't enough, and I rubbed vodka on her gums. I feel so much shame about this and hope that I don't cause her to be an alcoholic.

- My heart was broken, and I lost twenty pounds. I couldn't eat or sleep. It wasn't because of a man; it was because of my best friend and my judgment of the way she lived her life. That friend breakup was more painful than any breakup from an intimate relationship.

- I've been married for twenty-six years, and I love my husband. But I secretly hold a torch for my first boyfriend from high school. If he ever entered my life again (which is highly unlikely), I would have a super hard time ignoring it. He was 100 percent my true love and best friend.

- I grew up poor, beaten, and sexually abused. By the grace of God, I got into a good college. I am a Black girl and was living in a white world in the dorms on the East Coast. There was never a day that I felt like I belonged. I started drinking and isolating myself so that people couldn't see me and separate myself from others.

- My husband and I wanted to spice up our sex life so we had an orgy with all of his friends. We filmed it and watched it over and over. When I wanted to do it again and he didn't, I started sleeping with his friends on an individual level and didn't feel like it was cheating because we'd had the orgy.

- I had an affair with my engaged boss in my second job out of college. I was in my early twenties and developed a crush on my forty-year-old boss, who was charming and smart and successful and had an English accent that I totally fell for. And he fell for me. So, for months, he and I had a secret affair while he prepared for his wedding to his second wife-to-be.

- I hate my neighbor. I scratched her car with my key. I hate watching her leave the house every morning perfectly put together while I agonize over the right outfit to wear. She and I have known each other since we were kids and went to all the same schools. We applied for the same job. I was perfect for it, and she got it. I hate myself because of who she is. How did she get my life?

- I had a co-worker that I hated so much that when she wasn't looking, I went over and cut a plant that she had been growing in her cubicle and then acted like I had no idea what she was talking about when she asked me about it. I felt so self-righteous in my hatred for her that I didn't give a crap about her plant or her feelings.

- I got a call from the principal saying that my child had brought something inappropriate to school. When I went to meet with her, she handed me my dildo in a plastic bag and told me that when asked what he was playing with, he said it was a fidget spinner. It was my dildo that I had used the night before and had forgotten to put away. I was mortified!

- I stayed with a boyfriend who hit me for four years because I didn't want to go places by myself. We started dating because he paid attention to me so attentively. His attentiveness turned into control, and he wouldn't let me out of his sight. At first, I liked the attention. No one had ever loved me like that. I hope no one ever loves me like that again.

- I had two abortions, both with my husband. I didn't want the second one. I loved that unborn baby very much. I was too scared to be a single mom and lose the man I loved. I couldn't be strong enough to believe in myself. Thirteen years passed by and I eventually had a baby with my husband but left that marriage four years ago.

- I got reconstruction surgery for my vagina. I don't want to tell anyone about it but it was so dry, and sex was painful. I couldn't laugh without peeing. One day I was playing with my kid, we were running in the park and laughing. I felt pee run down my leg. I was mortified. Soccer practice was starting, and I had to act like I had spilled water on my jeans. I didn't even have water with me!

- One night I was getting ready to take the stage to receive an award from a non-profit. I hated myself so much and felt like a fraud. I took a bottle of champagne into the bathroom and drank over half of it. I tripped on the stage and can't remember how I got through the speech or what I said. I embarrassed the organization and myself. It wasn't the first time I'd checked out.

- I had a roommate in college who I didn't like that much. My girlfriends and I went to a club one night and brought her with her us. When we were ready to go, we couldn't find her. It was before cell phones and Uber, and we left her. When she came home the next day, she'd been drugged and date-raped. I felt so responsible and terrible that my meanness got the best of me and caused us to leave her. I was the epitome of a mean girl.

- I was so confused and lost growing up. I was starving for love and affection that I didn't get from my family. I began looking for attention from men. I lost my virginity at fifteen from a boy at school. We had sex in the bushes. What a horrible way to picture your first time! I had some serious boyfriends after that and ended up having an abortion when I was nineteen. I became a stripper at twenty-one then had a second abortion at twenty-three. I have since then cleaned up my life, but I carry that shame with me. I'm a teacher and a mom of two kids. I would die if this secret ever got out.

- I grew up really poor. When I was little, I wanted to be a princess and have someone take me out of my abusive home. When I got boobs, I started letting boys see them because they said they cared about me. This habit turned into me having sex. I didn't feel like I had any skills, and I was so afraid to be alone. I have been married three times and all three times I cheated. My current husband doesn't know or hasn't said anything about it. I married him because he has a lot of money, can protect me and I never have to be by myself.

- When I was in my early twenties, I wanted to be a writer and an expert. I had some early success and then nothing. I was in a position to be able to grade other people's writing. One of the submissions that came across my desk was so good. I was instantly jealous and thought it was my chance to launch. I lifted it. I took it, changed it a bit, used it in another format, and got it published under my name. Since then, I feel so much shame and know that I can never be a writer. That I'm not a writer. That I'm just a fraud. I feel like I don't deserve good things or true happiness because of it.

- I was seventeen when I began having sex with my high school boyfriend. My mother asked if I was sleeping with him. I told her the truth. She spent an hour shaming me and telling me no man would ever want to marry me now. She swore me to secrecy, saying my dad would kill my boyfriend if he ever found out (which was not the case at all). She then set about making it impossible for me to stay in the relationship and eventually we broke up. I carried her shame with me for the next thirty years, believing I was "damaged goods," not really good enough for a nice boyfriend who loved and cherished me. I am divorced twice and single with a track record of poor experiences with the opposite sex.

- I cheated (one time each) on both of my college boyfriends. In both cases, I kissed another boy while still in a relationship. With the first boyfriend, I confessed, and he accepted my apology. With the second, I have kept it a secret for my entire life out of fear of the rage it would have caused. But the shameful part is that those two experiences combined with the relationship with my boss have made me a cheater. That saying "once a cheater, always a cheater" haunts me. I have been 100 percent faithful to my husband, but I have had this fear inside me that there's a cheater inside me. I don't fear myself as much anymore; I've made it fifteen years with my husband, and I know I was young, but I sometimes worry there's a demon lurking in me.

ACKNOWLEDGMENTS

Writing a book is one crazy adventure. There are so many twists and turns along the way… and so many J-Lo videos. Every author has their secret "thing" that they do instead of writing and for me, that was watching J-Lo (Jenny from the Block, you've got it going on). Now you know my secret.

The process of writing this book turned me inside out. I knew from the time I was seven that I wanted to be an author and dabbled in fiction. I went on my own self-help journey is my early twenties and came across Iyanla Vanzant and Marianne Williamson, who both opened the door to help me gain a deeper relationship with God and a better understanding of myself. There have been other authors along the way who have touched my life and changed my path, such as Mark Batterson, Melissa Ford, Tara Schuster, Anne Lamont, and Steve Chandler. The wonderful truth about books is that they give readers a space to be able to connect to parts of themselves and pieces of the author all at the same time. The gift of connection, even in written form, is powerful. Thank you to all the authors who continue to sit down, question what they are writing, indulge their vices, write anyway, and then have the bravery to publish. It takes putting down the ego to put your private thoughts on paper for the world to see.

God: you were with me every step of the way and helped me to partner with you to write this book. My continued prayer is that it ends up in the hands of the women who need it. Thank you for using me to be a ripple for change. When I look back at my life, I see how all the pieces worked together for the greatest good. You are amazing!

Mom: I love you. You were the first woman in my life to love me, teach me, raise me, and pour into me. You taught me how to tell the truth and hold my head high. You honored my passion for writing and helped me fan the flame. Thanks for taking to meet Ray Bradbury. You taught me how to be a woman, question others, and discern how and when to follow the rules. Thank you for loving me and for gifting me with words, wisdom, and courage. I am forever grateful to you.

Dad: I couldn't have written this book without you, the crazy experiences, and your drumbeat in my life. Thank you for cheering me on, telling me to share whatever I wanted to, and even giving me permission to embellish (although no embellishment was needed). Thanks for letting me tell it the way I saw it, rather than maybe the way it was. I love you. Your prayers and love keep me grounded.

John: Come what may, my beloved. Wow. Just wow. Thank you for cheering me on, being my biggest fan, telling me I could do it, listening as I read you pieces of the book and showed you design art, toasting me with the most touching words about courage, and being big even when the world wants you to stay small. You are my best friend and the love of my life.

Jake and Jonah, my sons: I love and adore you. I am so grateful to the both of you for being my teachers. You sparked a fire in me to grow deeper in myself so that I could be more for you. Thanks for being patient as I learned how to parent you. I love the men that you are and am so grateful to you for cheering me on and celebrating me the entire way.

Tanya Chorn, my Eskimo: I never would have become a coach without your whisper in my ear. Thank you for speaking God's vision of my life to me.

To the women in my life whom I love so much: Beth Ann Burgun, Pam Brosnan, Kelly Castro, Sarah Jean Vick, Rosetta Willms, Melissa Klein, and Stephanie Bentley, and the rest of you who are my tribe. I love you. Your secrets are safe with me. Your friendship, laugher, and sisterhood have forever changed me. I love you all.

Marti Kartalian and Melissa Ford: thank you for being my guides, for listening to my secrets, and for helping me to see myself how God sees me. I appreciate your endless love and am deeply grateful for our relationship.

To my team who have turned into my friends: Kim O'Hara, Christy Villaseñor, Kelly Bartell, Olivia Olaguer, Juliet Clark, and Eric Franzon – I literally could not have done this without you. From raw idea to the writing, publishing, design, marketing, and edits - we did it! I am so proud of what we created and grateful to you for your part in this creation.

To the wonderful powerhouses who endorsed my book: thank you for taking the time to generously read and share your kind thoughts about why others should read this book. I was blown away every time I received an endorsement. I appreciate all you have done to get this into the hands of women so that they can break free.

To the mighty women who shared their secrets in this book: thank you. You are now free, and because of you, other women will be changed. To my readers: I love you. You are brave. You are strong. You are no longer secret keepers. You are free.

ABOUT THE AUTHOR

Considered by many to be one of Los Angeles' top coaches, Gretchen Hydo holds the highest designation of Master Certified Coach through the International Coaching Federation. She is a certified mentor coach, mesmerizing keynote speaker, and engaging workshop facilitator. She specializes in guiding individuals, organizations and entrepreneurs make high-level transformations by breaking the rules, shedding their secrets, and changing their lives.

Her coaching and wisdom help people step away from their default legacy and lean into a created future. Through these new lenses, her clients employ their very best version of themselves and achieve life-changing success both personally and professionally.

Gretchen is the author of the book, ***Break Free from Your Dirty Little Secrets: A New You in 10 Secret-Breaking Stages,*** and is dedicated to helping women break the rules and break free from their secrets to step into bigger living. She knows that when women's lives change, everyone's life changes. Her 10-Stage Secret-Breaking system takes people down a practical path towards their own inner truth and wisdom.

Gretchen has spent over 20 years working with individual clients, name brands, and notable companies. Before becoming a Master

Certified Coach, Gretchen founded a successful public relations firm, Chatterbox PR Ink. Her entrepreneurial experience, tools, PR acumen, and real-world practical advice have all contributed to the unprecedented results she produces for her coaching clients today. She has an extensive background in PR, marketing, and business strategy.

Gretchen is a frequent speaker, trainer, and executive coach at notable companies throughout the US. As a thought leader in her field, she is regularly featured in A-list publications, including the *Chicago Tribune* and *Fast Company*. Gretchen's coach training program for coaches, Stairway to Six, teaches coaches all they need to know about the business of coaching so that they can launch their practice and develop thriving businesses.

Gretchen lives in Los Angeles with her husband of over 20 years and two children.